TALES OF THE OLD U.P.

Copyright 1981
by Cully Gage
and
Avery Color Studios
AuTrain, Michigan 49806

Written by Cully Gage
Illustrated by Sue Van Riper Krill
Cover Photo by Hoyt Avery

Library of Congress Card No. 81-68104
ISBN 0-932212-23-9
First Edition - June 1981
Reprint - May 1982
Reprint - October 1983
Reprint - June 1985
Reprint - March 1987
Published by Avery Color Studios
Au Train, Michigan 49806

CONTENTS

FOREWORD

The stories in this book and in its predecessor, *The Northwoods Reader*, were originally written so that my grandchildren might know something about the way life was lived in the U.P., the Upper Peninsula of Michigan, at the turn of this century. Then as now it was a lovely land bounded on the north by Lake Superior and on the south by the forests of Wisconsin and the upper shore of Lake Michigan. It was also a hard land demanding much of those who by choice or circumstance found themselves isolated in its wilderness homesteads and little villages. They had to have *sisu*, the Finnish word for being able to endure all evils and yet survive.

Our little village of Tioga, located almost in the center of the U.P., consisted of two little settlements, one inhabited mainly by French Canadians and Indians down in the valley and the other atop a long steep hill where the Finns and Swedes lived. A straggle of houses and log cabins containing other nationalities lined the hill road that joined them. Except for wagon ruts, there were no real roads, but through the valley a railroad and the Tioga River ran, the former our only contact with the outside world. We had no radio or TV and even a newspaper was unusual but we had each other to talk to. Talk was what held the town together. Everyone knew everything that happened down to the slightest detail. It was not gossip, actually; it was the sharing of our lives.

And it was often very interesting talk, too because our forest village had the damndest collection of interesting characters you could find anywhere. I suppose that even cities have them too but in our town they were our close neighbors. Anyway, we cherished and enjoyed hearing about their doings and they helped us to make it through the long winter.

People have asked me if the tales are true. I've always maintained that they are fiction based upon my faulty memories of what took place in Tioga shortly after the turn of the century. If the language is sometimes salty and earthy, it was the usage of the time. We weren't very civilized in Tioga but we enjoyed our struggle for survival because we had a keen appreciation of the absurd. If you find memories and laughter in these pages, let me know.

Cully Gage

ROAST GOOSE FOR CHRISTMAS

Mother was just getting ready to hide the raven again when Mrs. Donegal, old Blue Balls' wife, came for tea. "Sit down, Emma," said my Mother, "as soon as I get rid of this dratted bird I'll put the kettle on."

When Mother returned, she explained. "I just can't stand that stuffed raven," she said. "It sits on the piano and peers at me day after day till I'm fit to be tied. Unhappily for me, my husband likes it and admires it and insists on having it on the piano. He likes to say, 'Quoth the raven nevermore' and it's his pride and joy. So I hide it back of the door in the kitchen pantry. Sometimes he doesn't notice it's gone for months at a time. And when he does, I just say that the moths have gotten to it and I've got it in a box with moth balls or I make some other excuse."

"I can't abide stuffed critters either," Mrs. Donegal replied. "Never could. Like having a corpse in the house. But I know all about your stuffed raven because Mr. Donegal sure admires that bird too. Says he's going to have one stuffed if he ever gets a chance to shoot one. I've been a-praying he'll miss. I hope it's expensive to have 'em mounted, Mrs. Gage. Is it?"

"I think John paid a man in Ishpeming twenty-five dollars to do the taxidermy," Mother said. "An awful lot for something that looks like a double-sized crow."

"Oh, well, then I don't have to worry." Mrs. Donegal looked relieved. "Bruce is so stingy he'd never throw that much money away on anything, let alone a bird. I haven't had a new coat or dress or hat for ten years. Almost ashamed to come over, Mrs. Gage."

Seeing tears in her eyes, Mother was sympathetic. She knew that her friend had a hard life with a hard man. B. B. Donegal was our school superintendent and he ran his home with the same toughness that he ran his school. His wife and children, his teachers and pupils, were terrified of him. Though we called him old Blue Balls behind his back, we respected him and worked hard to escape having our hind ends feel his heavy hand or strap. There was no mutiny on his Bounty.

But he was tight as well as tight fisted. He doled out one piece of chalk each week to each teacher and woe to anyone who asked for more. Old Blue Balls had been very poor in his youth and knew the value of a penny. It was part of a million dollars, he said. At home he was just as penurious. The Donegals set a poor table. I remember being invited one evening to eat with them and having hominy, a pickle, and a chunk of salt pork. No dessert! Walter, his son, with whom I played occasionally when he wasn't doing his interminable chores told me later though that usually they had fish and game, for old Blue Balls was a mighty hunter and fisher, spending most of his weekends in the woods or on the rivers. Walter also insisted that his father was really rich and when I doubted this he took me into the house and showed me a desk drawer full of pork and bean cans each one containing a big roll of bills, even some five and ten dollar ones. And a big tobacco can full of silver. But Walter never had a nickel to spend. Why, I used to have to give him some of my marbles so we could have a game.

When Mrs. Donegal started sobbing about how much she dreaded the approaching Christmas and that never in her married life had she ever gotten a present from her husband, Mother noticed me pretending to be reading David Copperfield in the bay window. "Cully," she said, "take those big ears out to the woodpile and bring in some sticks of birch and fill up the kitchen stove. Your father is making pills today so we've got to have the oven hot. Then go over and watch him in the hospital."

That sounded better than David Copperfield or Mrs. Blue Balls' woes so I did what she asked. In the early days of this century all the country doctors in the Upper Peninsula of Michigan had to make their own medications. "Some of the concoctions," Dad said, "were wondrous strange." I found him in the dispensary of the old hospital, wearing a white apron, and using a pestle to get the lumps out of a substance he was grinding in the white bowl he called a mortar. When I asked him what kind of pills he was making, he looked at me and grinned.

"Aspirin," he said. "Medicine is five per cent surgery and bonesetting, five per cent castor oil and calomel, five per cent delivering babies, fifteen per cent aspirin, and seventy per cent humbug. But don't tell anybody I said so."

The pill making was fun to watch. After the lumps were gone, Dad divided the paste into four smaller mortars and then colored each batch differently, stirring them vigorously. Next, batch by batch, he spread the drug on a marble slab, added some flour and cornstarch, and flattened it with a little glass rolling pin. It almost looked like Mother's piecrust. Then he took a scalpel and cut the aspirin dough into little squares about a half inch wide. These he picked up individually and, with a curious rolling motion of his thumb and forefinger, turned them into perfectly round little balls which he put into a wide baking pan and with his forefinger flattened them. Dad sure was deft. He made those pills so fast his fingers just seemed to fly and soon the bottom of the baking pan was covered. It looked pretty with its different sections of red, white, brown, and purple pills.

"Dad, why do you color them differently if they're all the same aspirin?" I asked.

"Ho!" he answered. "That's where the humbug comes in. The placebo effect. Why, I've had patients swear that only the purple pills did them any good. And damned if they didn't."

He was just cleaning up when old Blue Balls - oops, I mean Mr. Donegal - came in. I'd never seen him grinning before.

"Doctor, if you have a moment, why don't you drop down to my house and see what I bagged this morning. Shot four snowshoe rabbits, two partridges, and a spruce hen. Best Saturday morning I ever had. But what I'd like to have you see is the size of one of those hares. Maybe it's a cross with some domestic rabbit. Anyway, it's worth seeing." Then turning to me, he said, "And you can come see it too, Cully, if you want."

"Yes, sir, Mister Donegal. Thank you, Mr. Donegal." When he left, Dad carried the baking pan over to our house, put it in the oven, and told my mother to take it out in thirty minutes. "Some physicians don't bake their pills," he told me, "but I've found they hold up a lot better if they're cooked. Won't crumble so easily." We walked down the hill to the superintendent's house.

Mr. Donegal led us through the kitchen into the back shed. It was cold in there. Hanging from the pegs of a rack along the wall, all cleaned and skinned, were the carcasses. The biggest hare was at least a third again as large as the others. Dad admired it but opined it was just a big animal, not a cross or mutation. "But you'll sure be having a fine Christmas dinner. That big snowshoe might be tough though. Better cook the fowl with it."

"No siree! No siree!" Old Blue Balls replied. "We're not having any rabbit or partridge this Christmas dinner. We're having roast goose." He took off a burlap bag that covered a huge naked fowl that hung from a nail in another part of the shed. "Remember Doctor? I got that goose the last day of deer season - the same day I shot that Great Horned Owl. Got a deer and a goose and an owl and almost had a shot at a raven like that one of yours on your piano. Ah, I like this north country. Best hunting and fishing anywhere."

Dad was impressed with the goose. "Why, I bet that bird will go almost ten pounds. Some fine eating there, B. B."

"Yeah. The woman is going to stuff it with bread and hazelnuts. We'll have a merry Christmas this year, we will."

Most of the rest of this story I had to piece together from what Walter told me and what Mrs. Donegal told my Mother. On Christmas Eve she stuffed the goose and got it ready for the oven. On Christmas morning they had bacon and eggs for breakfast and Walter and his sister and brother opened their boot socks to find the usual five pieces of hard candy and the usual new book. But then Mr. Donegal surprised all of them. He brought out a large box with a red ribbon around it and presented it to his wife with a real flourish. "Now woman, don't you ever say again that I never gave you a Christmas present. Merry Christmas, Emmy!"

Mrs. Donegal was overcome. "Oh Bruce! Oh Bruce!" she exclaimed with tears in her eyes. Impulsively, she threw her arms around his neck and kissed him. Walter told me he'd never seen the likes of it before. "Oh Bruce," she said again. "Oh, Bruce!" Then shakingly she opened the box. Inside was a stuffed Great Horned Owl.

Old Blue Balls was completely oblivious to his wife's reaction as she stood there frozen in her tracks. "Great Balls of Fire!" he roared. "That's a noble bird if I ever saw one. Puts Doctor's raven to shame. Why you'd swear it was alive the way he looks at you! And that taxidermist did a good job even if he did charge me twenty-five dollars. That owl will last for years and years with some careful tending. Merry Christmas, woman!"

"Twenty-five dollars. Twenty-five dollars," said Mrs. Donegal dully as she went to the kitchen.

Old Blue Balls went hunting again that morning - to get up a good appetite for that goose, he said. When he returned at noon he was famished. Taking off his hunting clothes and boots, he plopped himself down at the table. "Bring on the goose!" She brought on the mashed potatoes, and the wild cranberry sauce, and the turnips, and the bread. And then on a big platter she brought in the Great Horned Owl, thoroughly cooked, pedestal and all.

"Would you like to have this carving knife, Mister Donegal?" she asked, holding it firmly and looking him straight in the eye.

I don't know what happened right after that but the next morning Emma Donegal emptied the money from some of old Blue Balls' pork and bean cans into her purse and took the train for Ishpeming. When she returned that afternoon she had on new shoes, new stockings, a new dress, and a new coat. Oh yes, and also a new straw hat with pink and blue flowers around its brim. She did not stop at her house but came straight to our own and had a cup of tea with Mother. She almost looked pretty the way she kept smiling.

AUNT LIZZIE'S MICE

In the western part of the Upper Peninsula of Michigan, the year 1915 is still remembered as the Year of the Mouse. Jaques Moreau, the oldest man in town, claimed he'd never seen the like of it in ninety years. We'd had a long warm summer for a change and mice were so plentiful we could get a sackful out of any haystack for our bass fishing whenever we wanted to. But it was with the first frost that they really invaded our little forest village. Out of the woods and fields they came in hordes to nest in our houses and barns and to beget more mice. They scurried across our faces at night. Mrs. Lappinen told Mrs. Niemi that for the first time in her married life, Toivo, her husband, had stopped snoring.

More barn cats became house cats that year than ever before but they soon became fat and satiated and so lazy they'd hardly open a green eye when a mouse ran over their paws. We found mice nests, all full of pink squirming little mouslets, in the damndest places. Mrs. Olson put on her husband's bearskin coat and got half way to the post office before she put her hand in the pocket and screamed. Two nests were found in the Town Hall's spittoons. The Sears Roebuck catalogs in half the outhouses in town had ragged edges. We shook out our boots before we put them on. It was terrible.

We fought back of course. When we flattened tin cans and nailed them over the holes they chewed in our floors, the mice always seemed to find some other way to get in. All they needed was a crack half an inch wide or a knothole somewhere. If we plastered these shut, the mice soon gnawed another opening. Hoping to starve them, our housewives emptied their flour bins into crocks, put their sugar and starch in jars, and their apples and potatoes in sealed barrels. All crumbs and left-overs went into the kitchen stove. Never had there been so many clean houses in our village.

And, of course, we trapped them. Flinn's store was soon out of mousetraps and couldn't get any more but fortunately our family had about nine of them so we did better than most. In our household I was the designated mouse catcher and got pretty good at it before the population reached its peak and declined. At first I had to set all nine traps three times a day and rarely was there a trap unfilled or unsprung. Sometimes I got two at a time. Don't remember how many I caught but there must have been hundreds that I buried in the strawberry patch. Finally the mice became harder to catch and I had to change my bait from store cheese to more attractive fare. The best bait I found, after considerable experimenting, was a paste composed of butter, bran, bread and bacon grease - and licorice spit. I chewed a lot of licorice ropes to get it and can't bear the taste now. Dad said it was the oil of anise that attracted them. Anyway, it sure worked and ours was the first house in town to become mouse-free.

No, that's not quite right. One of the French Canadians down town, Sieur La Tour, kept his shack mouse-free and it took some snooping by his neighbors before they discovered that his secret was weasel glands. Mice are deathly afraid of weasels so old La Tour trapped a lot of them, carved out their scent glands, and, after squashing them good in a can of tobacco juice, daubed the resulting essence all around the base logs of his shack. Unfortunately, the weasel population was far smaller than that of the mice and La Tour had already taken the cream of the crop so it didn't help the rest of us much.

The other house that had no mice in it belonged to a half-breed Indian trapper named Peter Half Shoes. It was a log cabin with plenty of holes in its moss chinking and dirty beyond belief. A perfect place for mice. And Pete didn't trap them either. He had a secret weapon - his pet skunk Mabel, his love, who slept with him every night. Skunks love mice and, unlike cats, they never get enough of them. They can eat them for breakfast, dinner and supper and still have enough appetite for several midnight snacks. So old Pete's cabin was another one that was pretty mouse-free - though it got a little high when it rained. One of Pete's neighbors tried to rent Mabel for a week but backed out when he learned that part of the deal was that he would have to take Mabel to bed with him. Otherwise Mabel would get too lonesome, Pete said.

Without enough traps, the future of our village looked pretty bleak as the mice begat and begat and the cats yawned and yawned. Then one day some unsung hero invented a new springless mousetrap and most of us found the path to his door. It was quite ingenious and easy to make. All you needed was an old water pail, an empty condensed milk can, some salt and a piece of heavy wire.

You filled the pail about a third full of water, punched a hole in the middle of each end of the little milk can, threaded the wire through the holes and suspended the contraption on the rim of the pail. Then you laid a board up against the pail so the mice could use it as a ladder, and wrapped a piece of bacon around the can to serve as bait. Incredibly the danged thing worked. The mouse would smell the bacon, climb up the ladder, jump across onto the condensed milk can and this would immediately revolve, dumping the mouse into the drink to drown. No work to it. No rebaiting. No setting or emptying ordinary mousetraps and risking your fingers. Just empty the bucket when it got too full. If it got so cold that the water would freeze, you just put enough salt in it so it wouldn't. Eureka! The Perfect Perpetual Mouse Trap!

After the ground froze, most of the mice had established residence in our houses and barns and the little mice factories in the woods and fields had shut down their assembly lines. The new invention soon reduced the mouse population so that our cats became hungry again. The village had been saved.

But I can't resist telling about one small skirmish in the great Mouse War of 1915 and how I contrived a better mouse trap too. One day I was sitting in my Dad's office in the old hospital when Aunt Lizzie, that old trouble maker, appeared and asked him for some poison. "Those mice are just driving me crazy, Doctor," she said. "They scare me silly. I've got two of them in traps but I can't bear to touch them and they've already begun to smell. And I can't abide cats either, even if I could get one - which I can't. They make me sneeze and my eyes water. I'd like some of that strychnine you give trappers to poison wolves for the bounty. I'll pay anything to get rid of the critters."

Dad said no very emphatically and when he suggested that she go rent Pete Half Shoe's skunk Aunt Lizzie left in a ten carat huff. "I was damned if I'd give that old she-devil any strychnine," he told my mother at supper time. "She's buried four husbands already and how do I know she's not setting her cap for a fifth?"

"Oh now, John," Mother replied. "That's not fair. All but the first one were lonely old men and sick when she married them."

"A hell of a way to make a living!" Dad said. "Anyway, I'm not taking any chances of being an accessory before the fact. Why doesn't that old biddy just breathe on those mice? They'd curl up their tails and die in a hurry."

I kept thinking about what Aunt Lizzie said about being willing to pay anything to get rid of her mice. Maybe I could go into the business. After all I'd been able to clean all of them out of our house, and the nine traps weren't being used, and I might be able to make enough to buy that old crooked-wheel bicycle of Mulu's. He wanted ten dollars for it which was too much but I had $8.23 in my little iron bank, the one you made your deposit in by putting a coin into the little man's upraised hand and having him put it in his pocket. Let's see. I'd need a dollar and seventy seven cents. Eighty seven mice! Might be possible. I'd caught more than that in our own house. So I went up to Aunt Lizzie's place on Easy Street. They called it that because it was the only street in town that didn't have a steep hill in it.

When she came to the back door I handed her the business card I'd spent an hour in composing.

CULLY GAGE

PERFESSIONAL MOUSE CATCHER
Satisfakshun Gerinteed
2¢ per mouse

I told Aunt Lizzie I had cleaned out every mouse in our own house and that I could do the same with hers. I said I had nine traps and my own special bait.

She tried to haggle me down saying my price was too high. At first she only offered me a penny for five mice, then a penny for two, than a cent a mouse, but I held fast. The turning point came when a mouse skittered out from under the stove and she pulled up her skirts, screamed and gave in. Aunt Lizzie sure had skinny legs and knobby knees. I went home for my traps feeling pretty good. I'd get that bike of Mulu's yet. I was in business.

When I returned I emptied her two mousetraps, set my own, and looked over the place. There were mouse droppings everywhere and I found a nest with five little ones in one of her cupboards right away. When I disposed of them and asked for my dime she refused. "No, no. I'm not paying for any babies, only for the big ones." Aunt Lizzie was tight. "O.K." I thought to myself, "next time I'll let the buggers grow up."

It was easy pickings at first. By the end of the week I had caught twenty-three mice and had found where they were coming in. One place was underneath the pipe that went from the cistern to the kitchen pump and the other was a knothole in a baseboard. A light snow showed runways going from the house to the garbage pile back of Aunt Lizzie's outhouse. Evidently the mice were going out there to feed during the daytime and back to the house at night to frolic, bed and beget. So I plugged up both openings.

Aunt Lizzie was sure hard to work for. She wouldn't watch me emptying my traps but she was suspicious that I might be cheating on my report. "How do I know you caught six today?" she demanded. When I told her to come see and she refused, I brought a couple of handfuls in to her living room and pretended to be about to put them in her lap. "All right, all right. Just mark them on the calendar each day. I guess I'll have to trust you but if I catch you cheating I'll go down and tell your father."

The worst thing of all though was that Aunt Lizzie just kept putting off paying me. When I bugged her about it she first said that she'd pay me after I'd caught fifty. Then when I showed her on the calendar that I had done so, she moved the quota up to a hundred "or until all the mice were gone." Just to be safe I cut off each of their tails with my mother's sewing scissors until she gave me a licking for it. After that I used my jackknife but I kept them in a can back of her shed.

After I reached sixty, the going got hard and I was getting only two or three mice a day, then finally none at all. Still Aunt Lizzie wouldn't pay me. "Your card said satisfaction guaranteed," she insisted. "And I ain't satisfied a bit. There's mouse droppings in the pantry every morning and I can hear them chasing around my bedroom at night. Drat it! I'm tired of sleeping with my head under the covers. You won't get a red cent, Cully, until they're all gone." Geez, she was mean.

But I knew she was right about the mice still being there. I figured there were about three of them left, one who lived part time in the woodbox that I called Shadrach, another that lived in the walls, called Meeshack, and a third who lived somewhere in Aunt Lizzie's bedroom. I called him or her Abednego and I almost got him with the stove poker once. Shadrach, Meeshack, and Abednego. Guess I heard about them in Sunday School once. Anyway, no matter where I set the traps or what kind of bait I used I just couldn't seem to catch those three. They were smarter than I was. Sure was frustrating.

Having snared plenty of rabbits I made me a tunnel out of birchbark, put cracker crumbs soaked in bacon grease at the end that went against the wall, and had a little noose made of one of the cat-gut sutures my Dad used for sewing up bad cuts. Aunt Lizzie scoffed when she saw it. "You won't catch anything with that contraption," she said. Then she saw me eyeing the cookies she had just baked and spread out on the table to cool. "Now, young man, I'll thank you to leave them cookies alone. I've counted them. They're for poor Mr. Dooley downtown. I hear his wife's in a bad way and likely to die so I think I'll take him some comfort."

"Oh ho," I thought, "so that's how Aunt Lizzie gets her husbands. Cookie bait! She's a trapper too." But I didn't say anything. Just went about my business until I heard her scream and call to me. I found her in the upstairs bedroom standing on a chair. Her wig had fallen off and she was as bald as an onion. I could hardly keep my face straight but then I saw what she was pointing at. It was a big mouse, probably Abednego, sitting on a hat in the hat box she'd just opened. I swear that mouse had the same look of shock that must have been on my face when I first saw Aunt Lizzie's naked pale pate. Actually Abednego looked kind of ornamental on that hat - better than the fake roses. I ran downstairs for the poker but when I returned the mouse was gone. Wow! Was Aunt Lizzie mad! All she could say was "Satisfaction guaranteed! Satisfaction guaranteed!" I got out of there fast. I knew I'd never get my money unless I caught those last three mice. I'd never get that bike!

I waited a couple of days before returning. The old lady had calmed down but my birchbark snare tunnel didn't have a thing in it though the bait was gone. Nevertheless I was more excited than discouraged because I'd brought with me my own new secret weapon. It was Dad's minnow trap, one of those long ones made of wire mesh with cones that projected inwards. Since I'd found a dead mouse in it all dried up, I figured that if he couldn't get out, then maybe Shadrach, Meeshack and Abednego couldn't either. So I pushed some bacon soaked bread through the cone openings and took it up to the bedroom.

Damned if it didn't work perfectly. The next morning I found three live mice in it and Aunt Lizzie said they'd been there all night which was why she had slept downstairs on the couch. "Then them critters just kept squeaking and running around in your cage all night. I couldn't bear it," she complained. "Hardly slept a wink." I was delighted of course and began to dream big dreams. "Cully Gage's Improved Mouse Trap De Luxe" - maybe I could patent it and make a million dollars.

It had one disadvantage though. It was hard to empty without having the mice get away and when my Dad caught me trying with a rope to lower it down our well so they'd drown I got another licking. Had to take the minnow trap all the way to Fish Lake. What would I do when it froze over? But it worked. The dang thing worked.

Though I brought it back to Aunt Lizzie's house I never caught another mouse either in the minnow trap or in any of the other traps. It was clear that I'd cleaned them out. No more droppings anywhere. They were gone. Finally, after two more weeks, I went up to Aunt Lizzie's house to total up the marks on the calendar and to get my money.

The calendar was gone. Aunt Lizzie claimed she had to use it to start a fire that morning and that she'd forgotten I'd used it to keep daily score of the catch. She had a sneaky smile on her face as she said it but it disappeared when I brought in my big can of mousetails and dumped them out on her kitchen table. "Seventy-seven, seventy-eight, seventy-nine," I counted. "Aunt Lizzie, you owe me one dollar and fifty-eight cents!" But once again the old devil refused. "I still ain't satisfied," she said. "I still hear squeaks in the night sometimes. You hain't got all those mice yet, young man. And if you don't like it, sue me!" The dirty old she-devil!

I picked up my things and went home mad as a wet hen and feeling very sorry for myself. I'd wasted a month's hard work. I'd been suckered good. When I told my Dad about it he was mad too but he couldn't help saying that it was a good lesson. There always were some people you couldn't trust, and everybody in town knew that Aunt Lizzie was one of them. Then he told me to solve the problem and to find some way to get paid. "And I'll give you a whole dollar of my own money if you do," he added.

Well, I sure did a lot of thinking and figuring for the next few days until I found the way. What I did was to wait until Aunt Lizzie passed our house on one of her daily evil gossip trips downtown. Then I took my minnow trap full of mice I'd caught behind Flinn's store, unplugged the knot hole and the place under the cistern pipe at her house. Then I let all the mice escape and there must have been eight or nine of them. I grinned when I saw that most followed the old trails right into the house. The next day I did the same thing.

So I wasn't entirely surprised when Aunt Lizzie came to our house and begged me to come back. I told her I wouldn't until she paid me - which she did right there. Better yet, so did my dad.

The first time I rode Mulu's bike I smashed it to smithereens.

PUUKO

 uuko was the blackest, biggest, meanest tom cat that ever roamed our forest village. He was also the most amourous. In the ten years of his short life Puuko actually changed the color of our cat population from grey to black. In his prime he terrorized not only every other cat but also every dog in town. Puuko didn't like dogs and most of them made a wide detour around our yard to keep from feeling his claws.

The exception was Pullu, a stupid old hound, who was a slow learner. Day after day Pullu would amble innocently down the sidewalk next to our picket fence. And there every morning was Puuko, crouched in ambush on the upper stringer by the gate post, waiting for his morning ride. He'd jump on poor Pullu and ride him like a jockey down our hill street in a satanic chorus of snarls and yelps. When they got to Mrs. Falange's house Puuko would get off, stalk over to her barn, look over her ten or more barn cats, take care of those who needed it - and sometimes those who didn't - then look for another mutt to ride home. And that was in the daytime when he was still dopey from the previous night's adventures!

"Puuko" (pronounced "Pookoh") is the Finn word for *knife* and it fit that big black he-devil perfectly. Puuko didn't just claw at random; he performed surgery, and every cat in town had been his patient - or paramour. My father, the village doctor, gave him the name after bandaging a long rip on my leg. I'd been milking Rosy, our Jersey cow, and had been a bit tardy in giving Puuko the squirt of warm milk he'd been demanding. Dad admired that long slit - said he couldn't have done a better job with a scalpel. And there was the time when Lempi, our hired girl, made the mistake of trying to sweep Puuko out of the way with her broom. He swarmed up the handle and slit her arm from armpit to elbow. Puuko, the knife! The meanest damned cat in town!

Even when he was a kitten, Puuko hadn't been a bit loveable. His purr sounded like an internal growl. No one dared pick him up and I was the only person he permitted to pet him - if that's what you can call it. When he occasionally rubbed against my leg, it meant that Puuko was commanding me to smooth his black fur twice - not three times - and perhaps to scratch his ears once.

The family probably insisted that Puuko was *my* cat because on one cold night I had opened my upstairs bedroom window and let him in after suffering through three solid hours of continuous caterwalling. It was a mistake because that tom cat slept in my bed every night thereafter. Except once, for a period of about three weeks, after Puuko's ambition had exceeded his discretion and he smelled hugely of skunk! I slept those three weeks with cotton stuffed in my ears. Actually, Pukko did not spend much of any night in my bed; he was too busy making service calls. It was usually with the first rays of dawn that he returned and sawed hideously away on that cat-gut strung fiddle of his until I gave up and opened the window. No, he wasn't my cat. I was his boy!

All of us respected Puuko but my Dad admired him, mainly because there hadn't been a mouse or rat in the house or barn since he appeared. Indeed, some of the Finns uptown and some French Canadian families downtown used to put out fish heads on their back porches, hoping that Puuko would hang around long enough to take care of their varmints too. He liked hunting rats more than mice; mice were too easy. Sometimes I'd see him up at the town dump behind Flinn's store indulging in an orgy of rat slaughter just for the hell of it, making the rock walls resound with his battle cries. As Health Officer, Dad said the village ought to put Puuko on its payroll. Did more good than Charley Olafson, our constable.

Besides his ability to keep down the rats and mice, Puuko also contributed to our larder, occasionally dragging a dead rabbit or partridge up to the shed door. These we ate gratefully though he always insisted on having the liver. Once he also brought in two of Toivo Lampi's fat hens for our Thanksgiving dinner, payment, Dad said, for the twin boys Dad had delivered ten years earlier but for which he had never been paid.

But the real reason Dad appreciated Puuko was the way the tom cat had taken care of old Aunt Lizzie - no relation - who was the town's busybody and evil gossip, always causing trouble. Puuko made his rounds at night; Aunt Lizzie made hers in the daytime. She was our town's newspaper but all she relayed was bad news, innuendo and suspicion. I don't know how many houses she stopped at to hand out the evil tidbits of the day but ours was not one of them, probably because she was afraid of Dad who made no bones about not being able to stand her. Said if she bothered us he'd give her a dram from the little black bottle on the top shelf - the one with the skull and crossbones on it.

Well, this particular morning Mother was out in the back garden when Aunt Lizzie came to our front door. "Young man," she said, sniffing loudly, "I would like to speak to your mother about an important matter." When I let her in, she marched stiffly into the living room and sat down in Puuko's chair. To my credit, I did suggest that she might find another one more comfortable but she refused. "Go get your mother," she commanded. "She's got to know what you've been up to!" For the life of me I couldn't think of anything I'd done recently that was bad enough to merit such a visit, but maybe I had. So I let Puuko in the back door.

When my mother and I entered the back door we heard Aunt Lizzie snarl, "Scat, cat!" Then she let out a bloodcurdling scream, bolted out of the screen door, down the steps and up the street, screeching all the way. We knew immediately what had happened. It had happened before.

In our living room, off to one side between the bookcase and the bearskin rug, there was a straight backed, red plush chair that must have been designed by Torquemada for the Spanish Inquistion's torture chambers. No one could sit in the damned thing for more than three minutes without getting a headache. I'm sure we would have burned it up for kindling had it not been Puuko's chair. Besides my bed, there were only two other places in the house that he claimed as his own - the warm spot behind the kitchen stove and that red plush chair. But they were his! Sometimes on a dare one of us kids would sit on Puuko's throne teasingly. He'd come in and stare at you for a moment with those green unblinking eyes of his. When red flecks appeared in them, he'd suddenly arch himself into a huge black monster twice his normal size, hiss menacingly, and snarl his battle cry. No miau, that! It was a terrifying "VVVRRAU!" Finally, he'd give you about two more seconds before swarming all over you, clawing and slashing. The warning sequence was always the same but sometimes it went faster than at others. No, we didn't play the game very often. It was Russian roulette. No one sat too long in Puuko's chair.

Mother was mortified when she told Dad that noon what had happened. "I've got to send Cully up to Aunt Lizzie's house with a note of apology" she said. Dad vetoed that immediately. "No you won't!" he declared. "Let it lie. I don't want that old poison'-tongue making this house into another way station on her daily trouble route. Good for Puuko!" And he gave me a quarter to buy the cat a can of salmon from Flinn's store.

Puuko's greatest admirer, however, was my Grampa Gage - though for other reasons. I remember one special evening that he and I were sitting on the back stoop watching the sun go down when Puuko appeared, preened himself, and sharpened his claws on the big spruce tree.

Grampa lit his pipe and took a long look at Puuko who was stretching his legs and arching his back. "Mr. Muldoon," he said, "some people claim that these damned tom cats have all the fun but they forget that it isn't always easy to be male. It's an awful res-pons-ibility, Mr. Muldoon. Now Puuko there would rather sleep in your soft bed some nights, like if it's raining or snowing. And I'll bet your gramma's garter there are moments that he'd rather just lie there behind the stove a-thinking of warm milk. But does he give in? Does he shirk? No sir, Mr. Muldoon. No sir! Night after night he'll gird his loins and travel the housetops doing his job in foul weather or fair - and getting nothing for thanks but more scratches. Lemme see. I figure there's two hundred odd families in this town, each with two to ten cats apiece. Call it four hundred cats all told, all a-raising their quivering tails in the moonlight and hollering for Puuko to come sing and dance with them all night." Grampa rose to his feet, clicked his heels and saluted Puuko. "England expects every man to do his duty!" he roared.

When Grampa went into the house, Puuko stalked off down the street and I sat there on the stoop wondering if I'd be man enough to be male when my time came.

As the years went by it became evident that Puuko was aging fast. Gray hairs appeared behind the whiskers on his face. He spent more time behind the kitchen stove and even returned to my bedroom before midnight. Some nights he wouldn't go out at all. He had sown his black seed with too much abandon for a new crop of jet black tom cats appeared all over our village, each of them full of his former fire. Puuko battled them one and all but from his torn ears, patches of denuded hide and lame left leg it was obvious that the old tomcat was losing more battles than he was winning. Little snatches of plaintive miauing showed that the old devil was hurting in his sleep. Yes, Puuko was getting old. He was just plain worn out. I sure felt bad.

Then an old spinster named Miz Altman moved into the vacant house next door, bringing with her a pure white cat called Melinda. Rejuvenation! I was with Puuko in the side yard when he first saw that white vision. His green eyes widened; he humped his back. And, howling, he made a bee-line for her. Miz Altman snatched Melinda up just in time and fled into the house. She was determined to protect her pussy's virginity as vigilantly as she had her own.

It wasn't easy! Puuko stalked her house and yard constantly. He lay in wait in the bushes by the back door. He hid under the steps in front. Once when Miz Altman had to take the slop jar to the outhouse Puuko almost got inside the moment she opened the door. Another time when the old lady was shelling peas on the front porch and holding Melinda close beside her, Puuko almost got to Melinda right there in her lap. One night Miz Altman just managed in time to slam shut the upstairs bedroom window when Puuko tore a big hole in the screen. Confined to the house, poor Melinda had to do her dirty in the parsley box.

Frustrated at every turn, old Puuko began to act strangely. He wouldn't eat. He wouldn't curl up on his chair. He didn't doze behind the stove. All he'd do was prowl back and forth, and forth and back again between our house and Miz Altman's. At night he never came to my window.

The worst part of all, though, were his yowls. They bore no resemblance to the mad housetop singing of his youth. They were single yowls but they lifted the hair on my neck. There was mortal pain in them. I asked Grampa if Puuko was sick - if maybe he was going to die.

"You're damned tooting he's sick, Mr. McGillicuddy. He's love-sick."

That night we had some real trouble. After all of us were bedded down and asleep, Puuko started prowling our roof and porches, really screaming. I'd never heard him so loud. You'd swear there were ten cats in a barrel fighting. He'd grab a high note, shake it, and carry it along the roof peak from one end of the house to the other. Even Grampa poked his head out to tell him to shut up. No one could sleep. Finally I heard my Dad get up and go outside. Then POW! Off went his twelve guage shotgun. I ran downstairs as Dad came in.

I was half crying. "Did you . .d-did you shoot Puuko?"

"No dammit," Dad replied. "Couldn't see that old black bugger against the sky. The moon isn't high enough yet. But, I tell you, I'm going to shoot him in the morning if he keeps me awake any longer. He's becoming a damned nuisance. I'm dead tired, being up on that baby case all last night, and I've got another tough day coming tomorrow. I swear I'll shoot that old reprobate before I have my breakfast if he keeps me awake any more." I knew Dad meant it because he was biting his lower lip like he always did when he got really mad.

For a time Puuko was mercifully silent but I knew it wouldn't be long before he'd be raising blue hell again. What to do? Frantically I rushed down to the cellar, got a can of sardines, opened it and started looking for him. He was crouched on the fence, swishing his tail, and looking at Melinda's door. "Here Puuko! Here Puuko!" But he spurned the fish and let out another of his love-sick yowls.

I remember crying there helplessly by the fence until I remembered what Grampa Gage had told me. Then I did something awful bad. I tip-toed over to Miz Altman's house, let Puuko in, left the door ajar, and ran back to my house to crawl shakingly into bed.

Only a few days after this old Puuko died. "Probably had heart trouble," Dad said. "Yeah," said Grampa. "Heart trouble and too much unrequited love."

Grampa was wrong. Sixty three days later, the beautiful Melinda gave birth to five black and white kittens. I felt it was a shame Miz Altman felt she had to drown them. Even if she did warm the water first.

WE TOOK CARE OF OUR OWN

Almost every child in our village went to Billy Johnson's funeral and we took turns tolling the church bells until sundown. Billy was the village idiot though anyone who called him that would probably have gotten a swift poke in the nose immediately. We loved that big gentle man-child. He was the village playmate. He was our own.

I can still see the big man sliding down Pipestown Hill on Arne's long home-made sled with three or four kids on his back, then patiently plodding back up the hill to slide down again and again, and always smiling in that curious way of his. Not a silly smile, either. Not foolish. It was a kind of secret smile of happiness, of contentment. Made you feel good.

Or I can see him in the summertime wading along the beach at Lake Tioga with a child on his back, two others clinging to his legs, and holding hands with two more. Billy never learned to swim but he liked to splash in the water. Or the sight of Billy (after he had helped us fill our berry pails) walking all over town with the daisy chain around his neck that we'd made for him. No one laughed at Billy for this. They just smiled. Perhaps they wished they'd had the nerve to wear a daisy chain. Maybe they even envied Billy for not having to grow up, for having stopped when he was three years old.

Billy Johnson's vocabulary was pretty limited but because he didn't talk much at all it didn't really matter. He would always smilingly say hello when he entered your house or met you on the street and he said it again for goodbye. He also said thanks. His only sentence was "Billy good boy," and that was spoken almost as if it were one word. Sometimes it sounded like a question and when we replied, "Yes, Billy's a good boy," he would echo it as a statement of fact: "Billy good boy!" He could say *yes*, but never said *no*, a difficulty that sometimes led him into trouble as you might imagine. But the word he used most often was "Work?" Every day as he wandered from house to house he would go up to someone's back door and ask "Work?" And if some chore was given for him to do, Billy was at his happiest. All he asked in return was reassurance. "Billy good boy?"

Since his comprehension was limited we had to tell him what we wanted him to do in very simple words, and to tell him several times, and to show him, and then to tell him when to stop. Mrs. Salmi found that out when she discovered not only her woodbox full of cut birch but also half of her kitchen too. (She'd gone to the neighbors to borrow a cup of sugar and forgot about him.) Billy was no good at weeding something like beets though, never seeming to know the difference between a weed and a beet, but when potato digging time came he helped a lot. Most of our families had him sweep out the barn or pump water for the washtubs or saw wood. Billy was very strong and he could saw wood all afternoon without tiring but he never did learn to split the chunks. No matter. In our land of "nine months of snow and three months of poor sledding" we needed all the help we would get with our firewood.

Billy had been less than a year old when his father, a miner, was killed. Some cribbing had let go an avalanche of rock upon him. Mrs. Johnson got a small pension thereafter but it was never enough to live on so she worked as the cleaning woman for the Town Hall and the school. She also took in washing and ironing. A hard life but she made do. Mrs. Johnson was a loving woman and very patient with Billy. Some people said she trained him like one would a dog. Anyway he certainly learned to obey anything he understood. He didn't know how to say no. Some little kids at times would command him to sit down, to stand up, to jump but since Billy always did what they asked and always smiled while doing it, such teasings were rare. It was much the same with fighting. If some kid (usually a smaller one who had been beaten up frequently by bigger boys) took a poke at Billy, he never fought back. Just let himself be hit and just smiled or said, "Billy good boy!" No fun, fighting with someone like that.

Despite his obvious limitations Billy Johnson had managed to get some schooling, if you can call it that. Indeed he spent seven years in the first grade under Miss Neeley, another kind and loving woman, and when he got so big there wasn't a chair or desk in the whole school that would fit him, they held a special graduation ceremony complete with a handsome diploma. Not that he had ever learned to read or write or figure or talk. But he could sure sit and smile. Miss Neeley said he was a calming influence, that just having him around made her work much easier. She missed him when he graduated.

I would guess that after leaving school Billy spent most of his time roaming our village playing with the little children or the dogs or cats and doing the chores of most of the houses in town. But then suddenly Mrs. Johnson died in her sleep. Dad said he had a hard time filling out the death certificate. Over work was the disease, he said, and Billy's mother had died of it, but no doctor would use that on a death certificate. So he put down "cardiac arrest," and let it go at that.

What to do with Billy? Only one person, Aunt Lizzie, suggested that he be "put away," be sent to the insane asylum in Newberry, if they would have him. Unanimously we agreed that such a course would be outrageous. We couldn't do without Billy. Suddenly we realized that he was one of the threads that bound us together. He had been the playmate of every child in town. He had done chores in every house in town. He was our own. No, we wouldn't send him away!

So for two years we passed Billy around from home to home usually for about a month or two at a time and we always made sure that he lived in one that had love and little children. Billy was no trouble at all. Didn't eat too much, always washed before and after meals, always said thanks. He really helped a lot and when it was some other family's turn to have him, everyone hated to see him go. Yes, we took care of our own. Or was it that Billy took care of us?

Only once was there any trouble. When Billy was living with the Niemi's, their oldest daughter with her four children came back from Detroit after the marriage had broken up. Billy had to move right away so Miz Altman, a retired school teacher who lived in the house next door to ours, took him in until other arrangements could be made. She too was a loving person and Billy filled a hole in her life that even her white cat could not. When it came time for Billy to move on she wouldn't let him go. "It's not fair to the poor boy," she insisted. "He needs a real home and I'll give it to him." So she went on the train to Marquette, signed the papers and formally adopted him. A few people gossiped a little about it, her being a spinster lady, even though she was old enough to be Billy's grandmother but we agreed that it was the best thing for Billy. It must have been for he even learned a new word. It was Mama. Miz Altman loved to hear it and lavished seventy years of repressed affection on him. She wasn't too possessive either. She let him wander from house to house doing chores and playing with his little friends.

Some said she was too permissive and didn't check up on him enough, and that was why the accident happened, though really it was Fish-eye's fault if it was anyone's. Fish-eye or Fishy was a French Canadian kid about eleven years old who was always getting into trouble or making it. Shorter than the other boys his age, he was the village dare-devil, climbing to the top of the biggest trees, tip-toeing along the upper girders of the railroad bridge over the Tioga River where it crossed the gulch. He'd do anything on a dare.

Anyway, Fish-eye and two other boys and Billy climbed through the barbed wire fence that protected the old mine pit back of Pipestone Hill. In our town this was the ultimate of all forbidden things. Everyone of us had been warned a hundred times never to go there, to keep away from *that* place. The walls of the pit were very steep and the water in it must have been hundreds of feet deep. It was scarey even to think about looking down into that great hole. Yet there was one flat place reached by a narrow winding route where you might be able to get to the edge of the water. The boys told Billy to sit down just inside the fence so of course he did. Then they made their precarious way down to the flat place. Fish-eye announced that he was going for a swim and couldn't be argued out of it. So, taking off his clothes, he dived into the icy water and swam around a bit, taunting the others to join him. Unfortunately he soon got some terrible leg cramps that doubled him up as he was swimming back to the ledge and in terror he cried "Help! Come help me!"

Billy heard him and obeyed. Billy good boy! Fish-eye got out all right but Billy did not.

Almost every child in our village went to Billy Johnson's funeral and we took turns tolling the church bell until sundown.

THE SINNER

ld Man McGee was trying to remember the Ten Commandments as he put the morning coffee on the box stove and laid out the hardtack. "Now put your mind to it, McGee!" he said aloud. "What are them 'Thou shalts'?" Though he screwed up his brow and scratched the white mop of his hair, nothing came except "Thou shalt . . . not make . . . any grave image" and that didn't make much sense so he knew he had it wrong. It was hard to think before breakfast when your brains, like your feet, still felt frozen.

The old man poured himself a cup of coffee and put some hardtack in it to soak a bit so he could chew it. He was still thinking painfully. Yes, it was tomorrow, according to the notice in the post office, that the big revival meeting was being held in the Methodist Church. The Reverend Cleophas Jones was coming again to the village. Ah, he was a good one. Full of hell and damnation, his sermons were! Nobody, no, nobody could really lay it into sinners like Reverend Jones once he got heated up and started hollering. McGee felt the excitement crawling up his spine. The whole town would be there, maybe even a few Catholics unless Father Hassel scared them out of it. A real doings!

But then the old man winced, remembering what a fool he'd made of himself the year before at a similar revival meeting. The whole damned congregation had laughed at him. He could see it yet. There he was a-kneeling on the ledge with the others and the organ playing and the preacher a-standing over him yelling at him to confess and be redeemed. And he couldn't think of a damned thing to say except that he'd once shot a deer out of season. Hell, there wasn't a man in town couldn't have said the same thing. That's why they laughed so hard. "No sir, McGee. You've got to do better than that! You've got to kerlect yerself some real sins this time," he said to himself, gingerly chewing the hardtack in the corner of his mouth where a few teeth still remained. "Thou shalt not . . . What was that rhyme you learned at yer mother's knee, McGee? How did it go?"

Gradually the words came back to him and he said them again and again.

> "Have no other gods but me;
> Unto no image bow the knees;
> Take not the name of God in vain;

Do not the Sabbath day profane;
Honor thy father and mother too;
And see that thou no murder do;
From vile adultery keep thou clean;
And steal not; though thy state be mean;
Bear not false witness - shun that blot;
What is thy neighbor's covet not."

Old Man McGee went through the list. He thought for some time about number three. He'd sinned plenty on that one with all of his goddamns but it would be no better than saying you'd poached a deer. As for the Sabbath, well, he couldn't think of how he might have profaned it, and his father and mother way back in Scotland had been dead for many a year now. Not murder. He didn't have anything against anyone. Adultery? Who would have an old coot of seventy-eight years - even if he could do it! Now stealing was a possibility, and bearing false witness - that meant lying - that wouldn't be too hard to do. But coveting looked like the best bet. No trouble with coveting - wanting something some other person had. "Start coveting, McGee! Covet like hell!" he commanded himself.

But the saying of it was harder than the doing. The trouble was that he didn't want anything. He had a tight log cabin and plenty of winter wood. Smoked fish and the carcasses of nine rabbits and one deer hung frozen in his shed. "How about the taters, McGee?" he asked himself. "Maybe you kin covet some potatoes?" but when he opened the trapdoor and looked down into the little dirt cellar he saw three burlap bags full of them still untouched. Plenty to make it through the winter what with his big slab of salt pork, lots of flour, sugar, salt and coffee. McGee scratched his head. No covets there! Why he even had some biting money in a pork and bean can, enough to buy another pail of Peerless Smoking Tobacco, and then some. Didn't need another pipe. Couldn't buy a better corncob pipe than the old blackened one he was smoking right then.

It being time to do his duty anyway, the old man put on his clompers (lumberjack boots) and went to the outhouse. Maybe he could find something in the Sears Roebuck catalog he could covet. That was always a good place to do some figuring - especially in the summer with the sun coming in the door and the flies a-buzzing round. But this winter day it wasn't so good. He let himself down on the hole gingerly and felt the cold boards trace an icy circle around his rump as he thumbed through the catalog from back to front. Wagons, no! Had no horse. Tables, no. Scythes and sickles? If he had them he'd be conned into helping someone make hay. No. Pumps, Pots, Pans. Nothing there. The cold was crawling up Old Man McGee's back. Ah, the Ladies Underwear section. McGee tried his best but all he could see was underwear. Didn't feel a danged twitter. Discouraged, he went back to the cabin and talked to himself.

"Well, sir," he said. "Looks like you just got to go out and do some stealing, McGee. Reckon stealing's a fair to middling sin. Nothing great, I s'pose, but bad enough so tomorrow they won't laugh when you tell 'em you done it." Again he winced, remembering what had happened the year before.

It wasn't as easy as he thought it would be. On his way to the post office and then to Flinn's store, he didn't see a thing worth stealing except a sled and that had three Forchette kids on it. Nothing in the post office either except the revival announcement which he read again. "Gotta have something to say when Reverend Cleophas Jones calls you up tomorrow night, McGee," he admonished himself. "Gotta have something to say!"

There was plenty to steal at Flinn's store even if there wasn't anything he really wanted. Nevertheless the old man had stashed away in his coat pocket three dried apricots, a box of animal crackers and a handful of nails before M.C. Flinn was at his side.

"I'll thank you to empty out your pockets on this counter, Mr. McGee," he demanded, coldly sucking air between his teeth and rubbing his hands. "Let's see. The nails will be eighteen cents, the box of animal crackers fifteen, and the apricots are two cents a piece, sir. Total forty cents, sir! Or I'll call Charley Olafson and you'll spend the night in jail, sir!" Old Man McGee fumbled in his watch pocket for the folded dollar bill that he always carried there so he could always feel rich and gave it to Flinn without a word. The storekeeper scraped the collection into a paper bag and handed it to him. "Don't need your business, Mr. McGee. Don't need your business. Don't come back."

On the way back to his cabin, McGee gave it one last try. On a big bank of snow outside Miz Altman's gate he saw a shovel. He went over to it and was debating whether to steal it then and there or to wait until after dark when Miz Altman came to the door. "Mr. McGee, I see you eyeing my shovel as though you wanted to borrow it for a bit but couldn't bring yourself to come up to the door to ask. Why of course you can borrow it," she said kindly. "Better yet, why don't you take it and keep it this winter. I've got a better one in the shed. Maybe you can fix that splintered handle for me and bring it back next fall. Help yourself, Mr. McGee."

The old man doffed his cap and thanked her as he picked up the shovel, but under his breath he said to himself, "A fine sinner, you are, McGee. You've got two better shovels in yer own shed. Sure tough trying to do some decent sinning in this here damn town." He went down the hill, carrying the nails, the animal crackers, the shovel, and trying to chew sidewise on a dried apricot. "Got to think of something to say, McGee! Got to think of something to say!"

The evening of the revival meeting finally arrived. It had warmed up a bit, to ten below, and a steady procession of people converged on the church, their footsteps squeaking on the snow. Five or six sleighs and cutters sat in the shoveled space outside the carriage shed while the horses that had pulled them, heavily covered with blankets, steamed as they ate their hay. Inside the church about fifty people shivered in the lamp-lit pews despite the red glow from the sides of the two pot-bellied stoves. A murmur of conversation suddenly came to a halt as the revivalist and a woman strode up the aisle and stood behind the pulpit.

"I (pause) I am the Reverend Cleophas Jones, minister unto the heathen and the damned, and this is my wife, Mrs. Cleophas Jones, who will grace us on the organ." As she went over to the antique to limber up the foot pedals and try a few honks, we looked him over. A gaunt scarecrow of a man! The Reverend Cleophas looked us over too with firey eyes that had the impact of a blow. Few of us could meet that piercing gaze without looking down and feeling guilty. Finally he broke the electric silence. "Play, woman, play!" he roared with a voice that shook the rafters, and the old organ boomed out with "When the Roll is Called Up Yonder, I'll be There." When only a few of us sang the words, he abruptly stopped his wife. "Sing, you sinners! Sing!" he commanded us in a terrible voice, his face livid with fury. We sang hard.

I still remember the texts he used because I looked them up afterward. There were three of them, all from Deuteronomy, and they scared the hell out of all of us. "The Lord shall smite thee with madness and blindness." (Deuteronomy 28:28.) "And thy carcass shall be meat to all of the fowls of the air, and unto the beasts of the earth, and no man shall drive them away," (Deuteronomy 28:27) and "The Lord will smite thee with the botch of Egypt, and with the emerods, and with the scab and with the itch whereof thou canst not be healed," (Deuteronomy 28:27.) It was the botch of Egypt that hit us hardest.

Deuteronomy was just for starters. The Reverend Cleophas then painted for us a picture of the damned in hell so vividly you could smell the brimstone burning, and feel the devil's hot pitchforks piercing your bowels. He let out screams of mortal terror to show us what we had coming to us, screams of agony that raised the hair off our guilty scalps. There were devils in us, he said. The same red devils who would torture us in Gehenna unless we repented our evil ways. Oh, I can't remember or recapture the terror of the scene as that gaunt madman beat us with his words of fire.

Suddenly he was silent for a long time and when he began again his voice was soft and cajoling. "Now, friends," he said. "I know you're saying to yourself that your sins are small, small sins, not really bad enough to go to hell for. Or that you've only thought of sinning and never really did it." The Reverend Cleophas gestured to his wife who came through with a mighty burst of sound from the organ. Again silence. Then he gave us a shot from the second barrel of his mouth cannon. "It's the devil in you!" he thundered, "who is thinking those thoughts. He's got you. He's taking you away. Down, down, down!" And we were back down in hell again burning, burning, burning!

Suddenly he was on his knees beside the pulpit praying for our rotten souls, asking The Lord to chase out our devils, begging Him to let us see The Light when we came forward to confess. The organ boomed out "Gathering in the Sheaves." "And Lord, when I, thy servant, goeth down among these poor sinners to lay my hands upon their evil heads, let them come forward to confess their sins and repent. Amen." Then he was roaming among us, up one aisle and down the other, laying on hands and collecting the first batch to kneel on the long ledge before the pulpit. The organ played "Come to the Church in the Wildwood. Come! Come! Come!

All of those selected came willingly, though as in a daze. All but Old Man McGee. His refusal infuriated the Reverend Cleophas Jones and he worked McGee over pretty bad, imploring, threatening. Finally, he got down on his knees and asked the whole congregation to join him in singing "Come, Come, Come!" to the old man huddled there on the front pew. Finally McGee gave in and let himself be led up to where the other chosen were kneeling. "Halleluja!" the revivalist shouted and the whole congregation joined in. "Halleluja, Halleluja!" They were all mighty proud that Old Man McGee had seen the error of his ways, and was going to confess and be saved. Old Man McGee having been the most reluctant sinner was called on first. There was a long silence and the revivalist had to really lay it to the old man before he finally spoke.

"I once shot a deer out of season," he said miserably.

CHRISTMAS, 1919

Of the seventy-five Christmases that I have known, the one I remember most vividly came shortly after my fourteenth birthday. The holiday season had begun very well, mainly because I had escaped having to take part in the Christmas program at church and school. Because my voice had changed, I no longer had to wear those damned angel wings that the boy sopranos wore at those affairs. Instead, since my younger brother, Joe, had to put them on and sing the solos, I kidded him unmercifully. Besides, there was new snow and the rabbit snaring was very good in the poplars down by the lake. Freed from school, every morning I'd ski down through the maple grove, then down the field and through Beaver Dam Swamp to bring back a snowshoe hare or two. I got so many that year I remember having to take them around to the neighbors.

But it was good at home too. Mother brought down the big box of Christmas decorations from the attic to be sorted out and restrung as needed. We would spread all of them out on the kitchen table, the red and green balls, the yellow lemons, the white icicles, the little blue fairy boats and silver stars, all of them incredibly fragile since they were of blown glass and very aged. My brother and sister were not permitted to handle them but I was, and so I gloried in my responsibility. Their jobs were to string the popcorn after I had popped it in the box stove and to prepare the loops of cranberries to be hung from the branches of the Christmas tree, jobs that once had been mine, and very tedious ones, with much pricking of fingers. The only ornaments they could sort were the little tin candleholders, each with a little spring handle that opened up its jaws when depressed. We used to chase each other around the table trying to pinch each other with them.

Then there was the making of presents for our parents all done in great secrecy up in the bedrooms. I remember that this was the year I made a calendar for my Dad, an undertaking that seemed to go on interminably, for I had gone to Flinn's store and for ten cents had come back with four yards of wrapping paper, the kind that the meat came in, brown and shiny. I spent hours cutting it into 365 squares with a day and date on each square and a little message of cheer. By the time I got to August, my brain had dried up so that I was writing things like "I don't think it will rain today" or "A long time to Christmas." As I recall, I never did finish the daily gems though I did assemble it and gave it to my mother to put in Dad's stocking. Which was probably just as well for I doubt that he ever looked further than the first week of January.

For my mother, who hated the long winter, I had prepared a sheet of birch bark full of violets that I had with some foresight pressed in the pages of an old Sears Roebuck catalog the spring before. I forget what Joe had made but I remember helping my sister Dorothy with the cross-stitching of a hot pad when she cried with frustration, being only seven years old.

Although Joe and I had long since discovered the fraudulence of Santa Claus, Dorothy had not and so we entered into the conspiracy enthusiastically. Yes, those little marks in the dust on the baseboard of the great pot-bellied coal stove in the living room were the footprints of the Brownies, the little elves who spied on children when they were naughty. "No, Sis, that stuff about Santa coming down the chimney and into the stovepipe is all wrong. Dad leaves the back door open on Christmas Eve and he comes in that way. Yeh, we've heard the sleighbells and if you listen you'll hear them too. So you'd better be good!" Dorothy's eyes would get wide and a delicious shiver would run over her. I remember my envy.

And of course we all left notes under the stove for the Brownies, notes that were always gone the next morning when we came down in goosepimples to dress by the warm glow that illuminated the brown isinglass. Each note always made affidavit of our virtue, whether we had been good or not, and contained one request, no more. We had long been told that Santa looked with disfavor on greedy little children. That year Dorothy's was for a doll cradle, Joe's for a pair of skis all his own, and mine was for a shotgun.

Oh, how I wanted that first gun! I ached in the bones for the hunger of it. If I got it, it would mean that my father recognized that I was no longer a child. Friends my age had them. With a gun I could shoot the rabbits and not just have to snare them. I could shoot partridges too, maybe even a deer if I cut the shell threefourths across. Oh, how I wanted that gun that year. When I hesitatingly suggested my desire my father had only grunted unfavorably, and the year before when I had asked for it in the notes placed under the stove, all I found on Christmas morning was a Daisy air rifle with a pump so weak the pellets often would just leak out of the muzzle. I was fourteen now and there was no Santa. Yet perhaps. Perhaps.

So I was very good those last weeks before Christmas. I pumped the water tank full to the brim every day without being reminded. Not only did I keep the woodbox by the kitchen range full of birch and kindling, I also split up a huge pile and stacked it against the barn. The horse and cow were fed lavishly and fresh lime was spread under new straw on the stable floor. I rubbed neatsfoot oil on the harness until it gleamed. I even cleaned out the chickencoop. I was good beyond belief. I didn't even fight with Joe, my brother.

Until the day before Christmas, when everything went wholly to pot! It all began at the breakfast table when Dad told Joe and me that we would have to get the Christmas tree this year because he had too many other things to do. I was overjoyed to have the responsibility. Maybe Dad was really beginning to think I was grown up enough to have that gun too. Whoops!

You might be wondering why we would wait so long before putting up the tree, but our father was always afraid that the fifty or so real candles on it would set the house afire, so he wanted a fresh green tree to minimize that real danger. Always we had three buckets of water under the Christmas tree as an extra precaution, and the tree was always taken down promptly the next day. But oh, those flickering candles turned the old bay window and the living room into a fairyland. "Now make sure you get a good tree," Dad said as we took the handaxe and left the house. "Eight feet tall and even all around. No dead branches. Get a good one."

Joe and I made our way down the ski trail to the swamp which was full of birches, balsam and spruce. How carefully we combed it, sizing up tree after tree. I even chopped down a thirty foot spruce because the top of it looked extra good, but when it was down there were too many flaws. *This* Christmas tree had to be perfect. We covered that swamp, my brother and I, and were getting kind of discouraged when suddenly in a little clearing both of us yelled at the same time "There it is!"

Unfortunately, as it turned out, we weren't looking at the same tree. Mine was a blue green spruce covered with brown cones, perfectly shaped and symmetrical. Joe's was a balsam, also a fine one.

We argued. Lord how we argued. "You're a dumbhead." "You're a double-dumbhead!" I pleaded with him but Joe was stubborn. I called him stupid and lots of worse names. I pulled the rank of my age and finally took the axe from him and chopped down my spruce whether he liked it or not. Whereupon he chopped down his balsam. Whereupon we fought until both of us were weeping. "OK," I said, "You bullheaded bugger. I'll drag my tree up the hill all by myself and you can do what you want with that measly scarecrow of a balsam. I'm not helping you."

Actually, I wasn't sure I could drag that spruce out of the swamp and up that long slope all by myself, and I was certain that Joe couldn't haul his, but I did it somehow, having to rest several times. At the top of the hill I looked down and there was Joe, just a little way up from the swamp, lying exhausted beside his tree, so I knew I'd won. But a half hour or so later, there the kid was in the side yard, putting up his balsam beside my spruce in the snowbank by the front steps, whimpering with fatigue, the stubborn little devil.

My father must have had a hard morning because when he returned at noon, and caught us hollering at each other and fighting savagely, he swatted both of us hard and told us to get into the house. The noon meal was ominously quiet and after it was over Dad said, "Well, let's go out and I'll hear your arguments and we'll pick the tree." I began reasonably enough but Joe did not, and within two minutes we were fighting again, slugging and biting and scratching and crying. Dad was furious. "All right, boys. We'll have no Christmas tree this year!" He picked up a trunk in each hand and dragged both trees back by the barn and threw them on the manure pile. We were devastated.

We were also confined to our rooms for the rest of the day, eating our supper from trays brought up by our silent mother. Dorothy sneaked up the stairs once and called us bad, bad boys - which didn't help either. She said that Santa wouldn't put anything in our stockings. I didn't have to be reminded. I'd blown it. I wasn't mature enough to have a gun. Merry Christmas! Although I was fourteen, I sobbed in my pillow and hated that bull-headed brother of mine. Merry Christmas!

That was a long, long afternoon and a longer evening, because in our house we opened our presents on Christmas morning. As I said, we had to stay in our rooms. Mother came up once to give me a hug and tell me, as she had always done, not to come downstairs on Christmas morning until we heard her play Stanley's March on the piano. She said that tomorrow would be a better day, but I was desolate. No gun. Probably no presents. Dad was mad at me still. And not even a Christmas tree! In vain I listened for the rustling of things being wrapped and unwrapped in the kitchen below my room, sounds that had always been there on other Christmas Eves. Once, only once, I thought I heard the slight tinkle of sleighbells but decided I must be mistaken. I'd even spoiled Christmas for Dorothy. No Christmas tree. No Santa for me anyway. I wept myself to sleep.

Suddenly it was morning and Joe and Dorothy were in my room tugging at the covers. "Merry Christmas, Merry Christmas. There's the piano. Hurry!" I fear I did not hurry leading them down the stairs, dreading to face that limp stocking and the tree-empty room and the look on my sister's face.

Then there we were in a room filled with a glory of color and flickering flame. And Dad, sitting in his old chair, with that crooked grin on his face. Not one Christmas tree but two - side by side in the big bay window. A balsam and a spruce. And my mother smiling through her tears. And a shotgun in the corner by my stocking.

FOREST FIRE

We'd never had such a dry spring and early summer. Usually May and June were our wettest months but this year only a few brief sprinkles had fallen, not enough to do any good. The forest floor crackled underfoot, it was so dry. Lake Tioga was down three feet and the Tioga River trickled through rocks that none of us had ever seen. The trout, usually scattered through the streams, were now concentrated only in the alder lined beaver dam pools. Indeed, the whole U.P. was a tinderbox ripe to break into flame. All of us knew that sooner or later some fool fisherman would leave his little coffee fire undoused or one of the trains would dump its ashes or send its sparks into the brown weeds along the right-of-way and then all hell would break loose.

Our little forest village of Tioga was especially vulnerable. Not only was it bordered on the north, west and south by woods full of leaves and downed branches but each house was surrounded by long uncut grass about a foot high, grass that due to the drought was already brown. (This of course was long before the age of the rotary mowers that now keep our yards green.) Unless the owner cut it with a scythe or had the cow graze it overnight it was more of a hayfield than a lawn. If a fire got going in the Buckeye west of town and we had a strong west wind, the flames would roar down our entire hill consuming every house in its path.

That was why all of us felt uneasy when we awoke on the morning of July 30th to find the sun a red ball in a gray haze of smoke filled air. Your nose stung with the acrid smell of wood smoke; your eyes watered. And there was a wind from the southwest, not very strong yet but then it always blew harder as the day progressed. Yes, there was a forest fire and it wasn't too far away, perhaps seven or eight miles distant on the far end of Lake Tioga.

All of us knew that sometimes under the right conditions a forest fire could run faster than a horse especially in jack pine where it would leap from treetop to treetop in a crown fire. We were glad that there wasn't too much jack pine west of town until we remembered the long belt of old spruce slashings that ran north from the lake to the mine. Lord, they were so dry, they'd explode! Once those old cuttings got going we wouldn't have a chance. Also, there wasn't enough water even to put out a grass fire. Due to the drought, half of the wells uptown were dry and for weeks people had been hauling washwater in barrels up from the lake on lumber wagons or going to the spring for drinking water. What to do? Take what valuables we could to the north side of the lake? Get on the afternoon train? Pray?

Even before Pierre La Font, who had been fishing for pike, ran up to my Dad's house with the news that a big fire was roaring along the south edge of the lake, some of our men were assembling at the Town Hall, each with a pail, a spade, an axe and two burlap bags. Some men, but not enough! Charley Olafson, our huge constable, night watch and deputy sheriff had his big silver star on his chest.

"One more man and I've got enough for the first crew, Doctor," he told my father, "but you'll have to round up another dozen at least for back-up when these get pooped out. We'll take three boats up to the dam and either try to hold the fire at Goose Creek or at the Huron River. If we're lucky and the wind holds from the southwest maybe we can do it, but I want the boats so if we get cut off we can go out on the lake and not have to chance it in the bush. If the fire gets over the Huron I don't see how anything can stop it, Doctor. Gad, I wish I had one more man right now. Oh, there's Simonen. I'll get him."

John Simonen had just come out of Flinn's store with his weeks groceries. A short, wiry but very strong man, he made his living cutting pulp and trapping. None of us knew him very well. He was a loner, living by himself in the old Niemi homestead south of town. Never went to church or any of the school doings. Never went to the saloon. Not much for conversation either. He'd shown up in our town about ten years before and since he seemed to want to be alone, we let him. Besides, he padlocked his shack whenever he left it and we took that as an insult. No one in our town locked their houses.

Charley Olafson went over to the store. "Simonen, you come with us now. Big fire up the end of the lake."

"No!" said John Simonen. "No, I no go. I too busy."

The big man grabbed him with one hand and lifted him into the air, then hit him on the side of the head. Not too hard. Just enough to make his eyes cross. "What you mean, you won't go? I'm the law. I say you go or I put you in the cage. Which you want?"

All of us kids knew what he meant. Inside the west wing of the Town Hall was our town jail consisting of a large cage made of latticed strap iron. Inside its iron door was a cot, a water pitcher and a slop jar. We'd often peered through the window to observe some drunk who'd been causing trouble sitting on the cot, holding his head in his hands. That was the cage.

John Simonen nodded his aching head. "OK" he said. "I go."

Charley Olafson turned to one of the kids and asked him to take Simonen's groceries back to the store and to have Mr. Flinn keep them for him. Then, followed by a mess of us kids, the twelve men carrying their gear walked down to the lake and got into the three rowboats Charley arranged to be ready for them. We watched them leave, four to a boat, two men in the middle each pulling an oar, until they disappeared in the haze. You couldn't even see the point around which they had to go. Too much smoke.

When the men got to the dam and disembarked, Charley ordered one man to row up along the edge of the lake to see how close the fire was and then to come back fast. "We got to know how much time we got before she hits us. Just hope we have an hour, maybe two." Then he stood on the dam and looked over the situation.

The Huron River that flowed out of the lake was plenty low but in most places, except for the deep pool below the dam, it was about thirty feet wide. Enough water for the pails and shallow enough so a man could wade through it to the east bank if he had to get out in a hurry. About three hundred yards downstream it narrowed where the river ran through a notch in the hills but above this the west side was mainly a dry swamp full of brown bunch grass, brush and maybe thirty dead tamaracks. Evidently beavers had drowned them some years before when they had a dam at the narrows. You could see the dry beds of some of their old canals down which they'd dragged their birch and poplar logs.

"Jeez!" said Charley. "First thing we got to do is chop down those tamarack snags before we start the backfire. They're the worst for shooting sparks and brands of any tree. We've got to keep the fire from jumping the river and with this wind those tall tamaracks will shoot off so many embers we won't have a chance. So cut 'em down!"

As the men started chopping, Charley went down to the narrows. "Oh, God," he said to himself. The hill ridge was covered with jack pines, with pine needles and leaves six inches deep. It was one huge torch just waiting to be lit. No chance to do any back burning there. Those jack pines would explode. Probably make a crown fire, maybe even a fire storm if the upward draft from the blaze got strong enough. For sure if the fire climbed up the ridge into those pines it would jump the river. Somehow it had to be stopped short of the ridge. Charley went a bit further south. "Not too bad there. Mostly swamp and we can burn that over. No, it's at the edge of the ridge where we got to stop it," he said to himself. He returned to his crew just as the boatman returned. "We've got about an hour, Charley," the man said. "She's a big one and coming fast but mainly along the edge of the lake. Not too far back."

That was good news. It meant that it might be contained in that corner of the river and the lake. Might be! Most of the dead tamaracks were down so Charley had the men start burning the swamp with one man across the river on the east bank watching to see if any embers came down there. Like the others, he had his pail full of water and wet spruce branches in the burlap sacks to beat out any chunks or sparks that came down. And a spade to cover up the hot ashes or embers with dirt.

They started the back burn of the swamp about twenty feet out from the base of the narrow's hill and then set little fires all along the south and west. The dry grass started burning immediately and was soon sweeping across it. Billows of smoke arose and in a few minutes the whole swamp was ablaze all the way to the river and the dam. The man on the east bank called out for help and Charley sent several men over to put out little spot fires, beating them into submission with their fir-filled wet gunnysacks or shovels. The cutdown tamaracks were still burning fiercely with flames ten feet high in the stiff breeze but fairly soon the rest of the swamp area was a blackened smoking desert. Charley ordered each of the men to throw a few pails of water from the river on the worst of the burning fallen trees. It did little good; just gave the men the hotfoot and covered them with ash.

That part being under some control, all but the man on the east bank and another to keep watch over the burned swamp followed Charley to the hill at the narrows. After putting out some little fires that had crept back toward the higher ground from where the burn had started, the ten other men began to make a fire lane at the western beginning of the jack pine ridge.

"We've got to do some digging here, boys," Charley said. "Chop all the brush and bury the leaves and needles under dirt. Got to have a strip about ten feet wide that's pretty bare so we can maybe burn up to it."

36

It seemed impossible to put a ring around that western part of the hill. Not enough time and the smoke was getting worse. All the men had bloodshot eyes into which their sweat ran stingingly. Their mouths, their throats were parched. Often they drank from their water pails or threw water over their hot faces. Sometimes they lay facedown on the ground to get a breath or to fill their lungs with bottom air that had no smoke in it.

All were terribly tired and the forest fire hadn't even shown up. "Each man clear ten feet by ten feet and then we'll take a break," said Charley and he shoveled furiously himself, helping each of the others in turn. When the first hundred feet of the fire lane had been cleared, he told them to quit while he went back to check on the first burn. It was OK so he had the two men who'd been watching it join the others.

Suddenly a burst of laughter came from the exhausted men. John Simonen was lighting his corncob pipe. He'd worked just as hard as the others, maybe even more so, and yet there he sat in all the smoke puffing away. "You're crazy, John" Matt Laitala said. "You're nuts!" but he said it admiringly. Matt went back to his jacket and brought back a pint of booze, passing it around. "A little snort right now is good for a man," he said. Each one, including John, took a careful swallow, not too big a one, before handing it to the next man. They were comrades and the feeling revived them.

"OK. Now we go on," said Charley. "Each man take twenty feet more and clean it up. That should do it." Somehow they finished the strip.

"Matt, you come with me and we set fire to the next swamp beyond," the big man ordered. "And you others, you get your pails full of water and soak your bags good and put 'em behind and along the cleared strip. Then take a rest. Maybe we can make another lane and burn it out between."

While Charley and Matt were gone, two highschool kids showed up. They'd hiked along the shore to see if they could help and they brought not only sandwiches but the welcome news that the back-up crew would be arriving within the hour. The men and boys were beginning work on the second firelane when Matt came running. "Come quick," he said. "We got to clear the other side of the hill or she'll climb and get into the pines."

The other swamp was ablaze when they got there and the smoke was awful but again somehow they managed to contain it. This time however, they had to fight the face of the onrushing flames at the edge of the hill, throwing dirt, beating the flames down with their wet sacks, stomping the hummocks. Finally, incredibly, they prevailed but their clothes were full of holes, their eyes bleared; their faces blackened by ash. They were so tired, they sagged. Charley Olafson was in no better shape. He was shaking but his voice was firm. "Well, boys," he said. "We've done our damndest. If that fire goes on the far side of that swamp we've just burned we're sunk but with the wind beginning to shift to south I don't think so. We'll corner the bugger right here. Fill your pails and take a five. Only wish we had a bigger lane or another one but I'm pooped and so are you. Let's go soak in the river. Wish that other crew would get here."

Just as he spoke, a big hill about a mile away burst into flame. Great masses of smoke, blown by the wind, drifted over the lake. Under them could be seen tall trees, orange with fire, shooting off burning branches or toppling. The men could hear it coming. There was a roaring, crackling sound punctuated by crashes. Bleary-eyed, but fascinated, they watched it come down the hill. Rarely did it make a steady advance but first one river fork of fire flowed in one path, then another in another, then both met and joined, devouring everything in between. Suddenly the swamps the men had burned and their firelane at the narrows seemed terribly small and inadequate. They looked at each other and then at Charley.

"Looks bad, doesn't it?" he said. "But I've seen worse ones. That fire's not very wide and it's blowing into the lake mainly. She's not going to get anything to feed on when she hits our backburn. Let's go widen our lane at the narrows and we'll fight 'er there. If we can keep it from getting in those jack pines on the hill she'll burn herself out."

All fatigue forgotten, the men grabbed their shovels. "Wait a minute, wait a minute," Charley roared above the noise. "Look! If the pine hill goes, everyone drop everything and head for the boats. And don't any boat leave till it's full or I'll choke the guts out of you. Hear me?" They heard. And they chopped and shoveled and scraped like madmen in that hot and smoke filled air. Half a mile away now. They scraped some more. When one man went down from fatigue and smoke someone flung a pail of water over him then told him to fill the pail and hurry back again. Somehow the lane was widened to fifteen or twenty feet, though now they staggered when they lifted their shovels.

"OK, Quit! Quit now," Charley yelled. "Go soak yourself in the river and your sacks too, then come back here and we'll fight the bastard all along the lane. Rest a bit. The worse is coming."

They watched it, felt its coming in the heat on their faces and hands, smelled it coming in their dried up noses and burning throats, tasted it in the windblow ash. They saw the fire divide with one branch flowing to the edge of the blackened swamp by the dam, then later another river of fire creeping its way to the other charred swamp. And they, twelve utterly tired men and two boys, in the middle, waiting and waiting for the fire to come to them. Two deer came first, then a coyote passing within a few feet of a man before bounding down to the river. Then a skunk, waddling slowly, and a scurry of mice. Everything was fleeing - except the men.

Charley walked along the thinly positioned men with no sign of panic. "Now remember," he said. "Your job now is to beat out any fire that jumps the lane. That's all. If you get it quick you can kill it. If your water runs out, shovel dirt. Don't put the water on the fire. Use it to soak your bags and use them. If you get too many flames to handle or if fire gets behind you, just holler and I'll be there to help - or someone else will. We can do it! I'll tell you if we have to head for the boats." His voice was husky and he coughed a lot saying it.

Suddenly the fire was in front of them with flames licking up the trunks of small trees, turning the reddened branches into gray ash before they fell to the ground. The very earth was afire; the heat was unbearable; it was hard to keep your eyes open; it was harder to breathe. Frantically, the men ranged the hillside beating out the bits of fire that flared in the leaves behind the lane. Twice Charley had to help out when too many spots of flame appeared in one man's territory. The big man flailed his bag and smote his shovel madly, almost with the strength of the insane. "We're getting 'er, boys. We're getting 'er! Keep it up! Keep it up!" He helped John Simonen put out a burning stump. "You're a good man, John. A damned good man. I'm sorry I had to tunk you this morning. Keep it up!"

Wordlessly John pointed to the right. A little spotted fawn was ringed by the advancing fire and was staggering in the smoke. Suddenly John Simonen dashed through the flames, grabbed the fawn and brought it in his arms through the ring of fire again, gave it a slap to send it on its way to safety, then ran to throw himself into the river to put out his burning clothing. "Oh, you damned fool. You damned fool!" Charley muttered hoarsely. "Hope the bugger drowns." But he was too busy smothering flames to care too much what happened. And he was surprised when after a few minutes John reappeared to start furiously fighting the fire again by his side. Charley noticed that John's hands and face were burned some but neither mentioned it. Too much to do. Too tired to talk.

That was when the back-up crew arrived and took over. They had plenty left to do but the fire had been turned back on itself. The original twelve men, utterly bushed, gathered at the dam, too tired to get into the boats. They lay there in the shade of the spillway for some time before washing down with river water some sandwiches. No one spoke. Then John sat up and filled his corncob pipe. "Any of you boys got a match?" he asked. In spite of their fatigue and burns, every one of those grimy, black faced, dead faced men had to laugh.

From that time on, John Simonen belonged. He had helped save our town. The men with whom he'd fought that terrible fire befriended him, fed him in their homes, took him with them to saloon or sauna, even fishing and hunting. They found that he wasn't really a loner, just a lonely man who had never known how to join a group. Somehow, it wasn't just that he had carried out that little deer in his arms or that he had worked harder than any of the others or that his face and hands had got burned pretty badly. It was that remark of his: "You boys got a match?" Grace under pressure; humor in hell fire. We liked a man who could say that.

39

HALLOWEEN

It wasn't fair! It wasn't fair to spoil Halloween with a curfew! Halloween was our night of nights and we planned for it all year long. When the village elders announced that every kid in town would have to be in the house after the churchbells rang at 7:30, we were incredulous. They can't do that to us! No monkey business on Halloween? No tricks? Why, it was as bad as abolishing Christmas. In vain we protested to our parents. We said we'd rebel even if Charley Olafson put us in jail, and we got lickings for saying so. No, the curfew was real; the church bells would ring at 7:30 and every kid would be in the house or in bed. How we hated the old folks! Couldn't they remember how it was when they were young - if they ever were?

Yet in a way we couldn't blame them. The year before we'd had the best Halloween ever. Hardly a window in town had not been soaped; hardly a doorknob had escaped anointment with cow manure. Some of the bigger kids had taken Flinn's delivery wagon all apart and then reassembled it on the roof of his store. The smaller ones had made the night hideous by running their spool ratchets on the windows or by knocking on the doors and then caterwalling insults at anyone who answered. Way back then in the early years of this century, trick or treating was unknown. It was all trick and that was treat enough for us. We raised bloody hell!

And it wasn't just that we'd made a pretty clean sweep of dumping over every outhouse in town. Or that we even had dumped over Salo's four holer with the doorside down and Mr. Salo still inside holding his shotgun loaded with rock salt. You could hear him hollering a mile away until his wife got him out and fell in the hole doing it. No, I guess they put on the curfew because we collected almost every gate in town and stacked them up so no one could get into the school next day. There was a pile of them forty feet high at each door; front gates, barnyard gates, pig pen gates. Why, we worked our tails off almost all night doing it. You should have seen how it was next morning with the pigs and chickens and cows and horses running all over town and people trying to find them and their gates and putting up their fallen outhouses and scraping soap off their windows and cleaning their doorknobs. Wow, were they mad! Old timers like Eric Saari said it was the best Halloween our town had ever known. Eric probably said that because we missed his shack with our devilment. Too far out, and besides he didn't have an outhouse. Just went down and did his duty in the swamp. Said he wasn't no chicken to be cooped up when he had to go. He was one of the few who escaped our monkey business.

Anyway, it was a sad frustrated bunch of kids that trooped home from school to be jailed inside our houses on this particular Halloween night. Except for three of us - Fish-eye, Mullu and me! We weren't sad; we were just scared by the enormity of our plan and the consequences that would ensue if something went wrong and we got caught.

We'd planned it the afternoon before in one of our secret places in the grove. Mullu and I would swipe eight clotheslines and knot them together and bring them to the side of the school below the open bell tower. Fish-eye would crawl through the school's basement window carrying two more clotheslines and make his way up the two main flights of stairs then up the ladder into the bell tower, fasten a clothesline to the bell lever, then throw the other end down to the ground. We'd join it to the rest of our line and drag it up to the top of the little hill behind the school. And then we'd ring the bell like hell.

That was the main plan. Fish-eye perhaps had the hardest job but he was always a little crazy anyway and feared nothing alive or dead. Also, since he usually slept alone in the cow shed, there being nine kids in the family, he could get away and come back without being noticed. I'd chosen Mullu because he was so big and strong and tough. Without him, ringing that bell with that much clothesline might be too hard to get it booming in the night. Also his parents were usually in the saloon or somewhere else. They were rarely home.

If Fish-eye and Mullu couldn't ring the bell by themselves, then I would join them, but if they could handle it, then I was to hide in the bushes by the school and be the scout. We knew that Old Blue Balls, our school superintendent, and other men would be there as soon as the bell started ringing so my job was to run and tell the other two when to quit and head for home. I didn't particularly like that assignment. Old Blue Balls always scared the hell out of me. Why, he'd kill me if he caught me - or almost, anyway. Also, I would have the hardest time getting out of the house and back again. My room was an upstairs back bedroom and the boards of our backstairs creaked and shrieked with every step so loudly that anyone in the living room would be bound to hear. Moreover, my parents rarely went to bed before eleven o'clock and our rendezvous was for ten.

My only chance was to climb out of the window, drop five feet onto the roof of the entry shed to the back door, then jump down another seven or eight feet to the ground. I figured I could handle that without killing myself but how was I to get back in again? Putting up a ladder would surely give me away. It was a problem that I solved by getting the rope that had once been our swing and hiding it under my blankets. I would tie knots in it and by anchoring the top end to my bed be able to climb back, I hoped. I also had nailed a couple of spikes into the sides of the shed to help me get over the edge of its roof. If all failed, I'd sleep in the barn with Rosy, our Jersey cow, and try to sneak in the house to pull in the rope before my parents awoke. It was sure chancey! The only thing that kept me going was the feeling that we had to raise hell for all the kids in the world.

I was sent to bed early, even before the church bells rang, because I'd argued too hard with my dad about the unfairness of it all. "It's time to bring a halt to this Halloween vandalism," he said firmly. "It's gotten out of hand. Be good to have a quiet Halloween for a change." I got a swat on the hind end to speed me up the stairs.

It seemed to take forever before the alarm clock got to nine-thirty and I could get out the swing rope, tie the knots and fasten it to the bedstead. Because there was light in the living room windows, I knew that my parents were still up so I had to be very quiet when I climbed out on the roof of the entryway dragging the end of the knotted rope behind me. The jump was not too hard and soon I was with Mullu and Fish-eye bringing with me all of my own family's four clotheslines.

Mullu had only three - all from Old Blue Balls' back yard, he proudly said. Fish-eye had two clotheslines joined together with a big rock at one end. He had unlocked one of the basement windows in the school before he'd gone home so all was in readiness. Huddling there in the dark and talking in whispers we reviewed our battle plans. Mullu was to join the seven clothelines together and lay them on the ground all the way to the little hill. Fish-eye was to enter the school, fasten the end of his two lines to the bell and then heave the other end with the rock on it over the edge of the school roof. Mullu would join Fish-eye's line to all of the others. I was to find the best place to hide in the bushes near the front door. Next, we would all meet on the hill then to see if they would need me to help with the pulling. I prayed that they would.

Again we rehearsed the sequence and decided it would be best to ring the bell five or six times, then wait for a few minutes, then ring it again and again until I, as the scout, ran up the hill to tell them to quit and get the hell out of there. As the two of them hauled on the clothesline very carefully to make it taut high above the schoolyard, I went back to the school to see if the ropes were visible. No. They were high overhead once they were tightened. I returned and told Mullu and Fish-eye just to try to get one soft bong before I went back to my bushes.

Lord, it was the loudest bong in the world! I lay on the ground there in the darkness absolutely petrified. Bong, bong, bong, bong, bong! Then silence. Then bong, bong, bong again. I heard a man come running up to the school door around the corner from where I hid and the rattle of a key in the lock. Bong, bong, bong! And then I heard Old Blue Balls' terrible voice. "Stop it!" he roared. "I'll tan your tarnel hides so you'll not sit down till spring. Stop it this instant!" Bong, bong, bong, bong went the bell. I could hear Old Blue Balls running up and down the stairs in the darkness hollering till he made the walls vibrate. And the hair on my back too! Oh, he was mad! Another silence and then another bonging as the superintendent emerged. "Got to get a light! Got to get a light! That young devil's hiding in there somewhere pulling the bellrope."

Two other men, one with a carbide bullseye lantern, ran up to meet him. To my horror, one of them was my father and the other Charley Olafson, the night watch and jailor. I buried my nose in the dirt like a worm, as I heard Blue Balls explain. "There's a damned kid in there who's been . . ." Bong, bong, bong, bong, bong! "Who's been ringing that damned bell. You know how the bellrope runs down those holes in the three floors from the belfry to the basement. Well, when I searched one floor, he must have run down to another and started ringing it . . ." Bong, bong, bong, bong, bong!

I was even too scared to grin, being no more than fifteen feet from where they stood talking. Then they made their plans. Charley and the superintendent would start at the basement and search all three floors one by one as my dad guarded the back door and the fire escape. Bong bong, bong! There under the bush I groveled in terror as my father passed not four feet from where I lay. It was time to quit. Shakingly I ran in the darkness around the other side of the school and up to where Mullu and Fish-eye were still heaving at the rope. "Lemme have one good pull!" I said breathlessly and in all my days I've never known such satisfaction as when that old bell boomed over the valley. Any more would have been a vulgar indulgence so, after shaking hands and hugging each other, we parted and went home. The silence was deafening.

It took me a couple of tries before I made it up the rope and into my bedroom. I had just untied the knots and hid the rope in an old sweater in the closet when my father returned. I could hear him talking to Mother in the kitchen and the clink of a spoon against a bowl as he had some bread and milk. I also heard him mention my name and the room seemed suddenly full of alarm bells. "No, John," my mother said, "Cully's been here all the time. You know how hard he sleeps. Why, he didn't even hear all that bell ringing, or he'd been down here asking what it was for." Nevertheless in a minute or two the steps of the backstairs squeaked heavily as my father looked in my room to see if indeed I was in bed. He knew me! I sure was in bed and I made my breathing nice and easy-like until he went away. When I finally did go to sleep, I was reciting over and over again that old poem we had to memorize in the fifth grade about "Curfew shall not ring tonight." It had been a good Halloween after all.

THE TANK

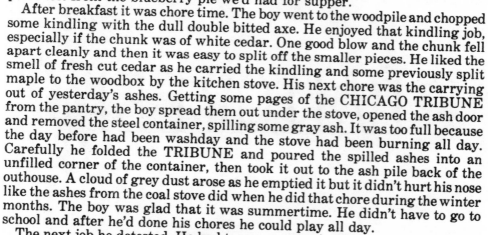

I t was seven o'clock and time to get up for the boy had just heard his father open the back door under his bedroom, to out on the stoop and blow his nose. A mighty blast, that. The neighbors could set their watches by it. Dad didn't believe in handkerchiefs except when we had company. He took his nose between thumb and forefinger and blew it free. Said that a rich man put in his pocket what a poor man threw away. Anyway it was time to go down to breakfast. Maybe there'd be another piece left from the blueberry pie we'd had for supper.

After breakfast it was chore time. The boy went to the woodpile and chopped some kindling with the dull double bitted axe. He enjoyed that kindling job, especially if the chunk was of white cedar. One good blow and the chunk fell apart cleanly and then it was easy to split off the smaller pieces. He liked the smell of fresh cut cedar as he carried the kindling and some previously split maple to the woodbox by the kitchen stove. His next chore was the carrying out of yesterday's ashes. Getting some pages of the CHICAGO TRIBUNE from the pantry, the boy spread them out under the stove, opened the ash door and removed the steel container, spilling some gray ash. It was too full because the day before had been washday and the stove had been burning all day. Carefully he folded the TRIBUNE and poured the spilled ashes into an unfilled corner of the container, then took it out to the ash pile back of the outhouse. A cloud of grey dust arose as he emptied it but it didn't hurt his nose like the ashes from the coal stove did when he did that chore during the winter months. The boy was glad that it was summertime. He didn't have to go to school and after he'd done his chores he could play all day.

The next job he detested. He had to pump water into the old oak watertank upstairs. His was the only house in town that had running water in the faucets; all the others had to draw up pails of water from their wells. Maybe that was easier than all the pumping he had to do every day. The boy went up the backstairs to see how far down the water level was. Oh, oh! Almost empty. Phew, that would mean 800 strokes of the pump handle down in the kitchen, an eternity of pumping. After pumping 200 strokes the boy's arms began to ache so he went upstairs again. Lord, he could barely see the water. Someday, when his folks were gone, he'd take a brace and bit and bore a hole in the kitchen ceiling, make a float and run a string over some spool pulleys by the tank then down into the kitchen right by the pump, put a weight on the end of the string and make marks on the wall to show how full the tank was. A good idea but his father would give him a good licking if he ever tried it.

Two hundred thirty, two hundred thirty-one, two hundred thirty-two. The boy's arms ached. Four hundred seventy-seven, four hundred seventy-eight; his arms were getting paralyzed. If they fell off, his folks would be sorry but he wouldn't ever have to pump that damned tank full again. Maybe there was another leak in the old wood tank. He checked but no, no leak. Four hundred ninety-nine, five hundred. The boy went upstairs again. Now he could see the water level. The tank was half full. Someday he'd get a steam engine to run the pump like they had at the mine. "Nuts, I'll do the rest of it later. I've got other chores to do."

Rosie, the Jersey cow, had been kept in for a few days because of a sore leg but it had healed and the boy let her out of the barn, opened the big swinging gate, and followed her up the street to the gate that blocked the lane through the grove to the big pasture field. Rosie walked very slowly swinging her bag back and forth and she knew where to go. Impatient, the boy slapped her on the back but it didn't do any good. Just hurt his hand. Cows always took their time. You couldn't hurry them. He thought of just letting Rosie find her way to the pasture by herself but then he remembered his father's admonition. Don't let her stay in the grove or she might eat some of the blue aconite berries in the woods and die. So the boy followed her down to the field and waited till the cow began to grub and munch the grass.

Returning, he cleaned out her stanchion, putting the mess around the rhubarb this time for the boy loved the rhubarb and sugar plum pie his mother baked. Soon the sugar plums would be ripening all over the forest clearings. They were fun to pick too. You could strip them off the big bushes a handful at a time with no stooping. Just had to watch out for the bears who loved them too. The boy could almost smell that pie with the pink juice leaking through the fork holes in the crust. He went into the house and pumped again. One hundred more pumps, two hundred more to go. It was time to clean the horse's box stall. The boy didn't mind doing it even though the ammonia smell of the manure was rank. Billy was his horse, his love. "I wish Dad didn't have to use him on his morning and afternoon calls so often. Maybe, this afternoon I can have him all to myself and ride him down to Lake Tioga or up to Rock Dam if he isn't too tired out." The boy scraped the box stall clean, scattered lime over the floor and put down fresh straw. Then he dug a few carrots from the garden to put with Billy's oats in the feedbox.

What next? "Oh, yes, the tank. Have to finish pumping it before Dad gets back." But the boy couldn't bear to tackle it just then. Instead, he went to the chicken coop and gathered the eggs, brown ones from the Rhode Island Reds and white ones from the Leghorns, finding four of each. One white one was huge, a double yolker. "Bet that made her holler," he thought. The boy hefted the burlap sack in which the broody hen was hung. She didn't squawk or move. "Still broody. No sense taking her out now. Maybe tomorrow." Since one of the nests was getting pretty thin, he put some more straw in it, then filled the feeder with scratch feed and put fresh water in the pans. His father had asked him to check to see if the coop needed cleaning. It did all right. The winter's leaves and straw were caked in layers on the floor and the place smelled pretty strong but cleaning the coop would take almost a day's work so the boy just put some more straw over the old stuff. Besides it looked like it might rain maybe and you couldn't finish cleaning it when all the hens were in there with you. Feeling a bit guilty, the boy got some haywire and patched the hole in the chicken wire fence where the skunk got in one night and also the upper hole where the partridge had killed itself the fall before during the Mad Moon when they went crazy.

The boy felt tired so he returned to the house and went down to the cool cellar with a glass and a spoon, using the latter to push back the thick cream from the big bowl so he could dip out the milk. Then he got a big cartwheel sugar cookie from the jar in the pantry and sat down with his milk on the back stoop for his midmorning snack.

Back to work at the pumping! Six hundred and one, six hundred and two, six hundred and three. Would he ever get done? He climbed the backstairs again. Jeez, it would take 150 more strokes at least just to bring the water up to the upper plank that was kind of rotten. His father had said never to have the water level so it touched that place. "I ain't big enough to have to do all this pumping, I'm only ten years old going on eleven," the boy said to himself resentfully. "Why did Dad have to take a bath last night after mother used so much water for her washtubs? It wasn't fair." At 698 strokes the boy had to quit. Couldn't even get two more. He heard his mother filling the teakettle and begrudged the act. Filling that kettle meant ten more pumps probably, and he told her so. "Well, Cully," she answered, "why don't you quit for a while and bring in a cake of ice for the icebox instead? We're about out. And have another cookie to take along."

The icehouse was a fairly large square shed behind the barn. It had double walls with the space between them filled with shredded charcoal from the old kilns. In the old days, they used the charcoal in the big stone furnace by the waterfall to melt the iron ore into pig iron, the boy remembered. And he also recalled with pleasure how his father had taken him down to Lake Tioga when the men were cutting the ice the winter before. How two men with a long crosscut would saw out the four by two foot chunks of blue ice, fasten big tongs and then have a horse pull the ice blocks up a snow ramp and onto the empty sleigh. And the boy also remembered how the next day his Dad had taken him back down to the place and they had caught a lot of lawyers (ling; landlocked cod). Not much fight to them even though they were about two feet long. They froze right away in the snow. His mother never liked to cook lawyers because, even though dead, they kicked around in the frying pan as though they weren't. Just reflex action, his father said, and they were fine eating. Good to have fresh fish rather than smoked ones for a change when the snows were deep on the land.

The boy unlocked the big heavy door to the icehouse and swung it open. Very cool in there but he got up a sweat uncovering the sawdust from a long chunk and prying it loose with a crowbar, then sawing it into three pieces. The house icebox, if empty, always took two of these smaller blocks. You didn't have to make the cut all the way through with the saw - just go down about three inches then put the axe blade in the cut and hit it hard with the crowbar. He liked the way it split open and left some chips of ice for him to suck. Cool on the tongue! The boy put one of the three cut chunks back in the icehouse and covered it with sawdust and shut the door tight. Then came the hard work of getting the chunks - must weigh 25 pounds apiece, he thought - into the wheelbarrow. Pretty heavy but he managed it. The boy sat down and sucked some more ice before wheeling the iceblocks over to the barn well about fifty feet away. You always had to wash down the chunks so they'd be free from any sawdust or dirt before putting them in the icebox in the house. That was the rule!

Getting water out of the barn well was more fun than pumping but it took a certain knack. You first had to unwind the rope from the windlass and hang it in loose loops from the circular stone wall bordering the well so that it could fall free. Then you took the bucket and dropped it, open end down, into the dark water below. If you did it just right, the bucket would fill up instantly; if you didn't, you had to try and try again. Then you turned the crank on the windlass around and around until the bucket broke the surface and came up

46

where it could be reached. There was a tricky moment then, too. The crank handle had to be held with one hand while you grabbed the bucket with the other at the same time. Sometimes the bucket slipped and down the pail went again, the windless handle revolving so fast that it would break an arm if it hit you. But the boy enjoyed the challenge and soon the ice cakes were clean enough to take to the house and put them in the zinc lined chambers of the ice chest.

The boy was pooped and so he sat down for a time at the edge of the sandpile, noting dully that his little brother had messed up the play iron mine he'd constructed the afternoon before. He was too tired to care much. But the tank had to be filled before noon and the eleven-thirty train was whistling down in the valley so the boy started pumping again. Seven hundred fifty-two . . . seven hundred eighty-five. Upstairs the boy went again. Yeah, almost full at last. Fifty more strokes should do it.

Somehow they got done just as his father entered the kitchen door. "Cully," he said, "I'm tired. Unhitch Billy from the buckboard and feed and water him. He's tired and hungry too. I trotted him back all the way from Halfway so I could be sure to get here in time for dinner. Now, water him good before you give him the oats." The boy went back to the barn well and it took three pails before Billy quit drinking and could have his oats.

The family was almost through dinner when the boy sat down to the table. He felt almost too tired to begin to eat but once he did, he found he was very hungry. Or at least until he heard his father say, "Edyth, after you do the dishes, open all the faucets. I just heard that this morning the new steel water tank I sent for is down at the depot and Marchland will be bringing it up soon. I got Charley Olafson and another couple of men to help bring it upstairs and install it after they tear out the old oak tank."

The boy was suddenly too tired even to taste his apple pie.

HE HUNG HIMSELF TO THE MAPLE TREE

Dad was feeling very good as he finished the last bite of cheese that went with the apple pie. A good supper. "Madam, you have acquired merit!" he said to my mother as he settled himself down in the big Morris chair and lit his evening cigar. It had been a long hard day. As the only physician in a forested territory as large as the state of Rhode Island, he had spent the morning traveling via freight train caboose to Sidnaw and back, the afternoon making local house calls via horse and buckboard, and soon it would be time to go across the street to his office in the old hospital for another three hours.

That's why he was so irritated when he heard a knock at the door. "Another wart! I'll give him short shrift. Why can't they wait till office hours!" He was biting his lower lip as he opened the door. It was Gervais Lafollette, a big French-Canadian kid from downtown. One of his eyes was swollen shut and there was a big purple and red bruise on one cheek. Dad gave him his short shrift. "So you've been fighting with the Finns again. Well, you go over and sit on the hospital steps and I'll come over when I've finished my supper. You ought to know better than to come at this time!" Dad slammed the door.

But he hardly had time to light his cigar again when Gervais opened the door. Didn't even knock. "No, no, Doctor. Not me. Not me. It's my father. He's hung himself. Come quick. He said he was going to hang himself and he did. Ma mere, she say run up and get the doctor. Please!"

When Dad returned about an hour later he went to the wall phone in the front hall, cranked it a couple of times, then said to the operator, "Millie, call Father Hassel and the undertaker and tell them they'd better get down to Lafollette's place as soon as they can . . . Yeah, suicide . . . Hung himself."

Dad went back to his Morris chair and smoked his cigar for awhile while Mother and I waited expectantly. He was thinking hard. Finally he spoke.

"Well, I suppose I might as well tell you. News like that sure travels fast. Millie had already heard it and the body was still warm when I got there.

Anyway, I guess it was Pierre Lacotte who found him still kicking a little and let him down from the chain-fall but he was dead when I got there. Evidently, Lafollette had tied the noose-rope to the chain-fall, raised an old ladder against the maple tree, tied the chain-fall to a limb and cranked it up, put the noose around his neck, then kicked over the ladder."

"What's a chain-fall?" asked my mother.

"Oh, it's like a block and tackle sort of, except that it uses a chain. You can lift a ton with it using just one hand. I suppose he stole it from the mine shop that time they had the break-in after the mine shut down. Anyway, it worked. Lafollette's dead as a doornail. Wonder what his wife and kids are going to do now? Not that he ever took very good care of them at that - always drinking and fighting and screwing around.

"How old was he?"

"Let's see. Oh, yes. I delivered his first boy, Gervais, the year of the big storm. He's the one who came to the door to get me. Let me see. Gervais must be fifteen. Oh, I'd say Lafollette must have been thirty-five or thirty-six."

"What a shame!" said my mother.

"No," replied Dad. "He was a no good just like his father and his grandfather before him. Grandpere Lafollette spent time in prison for killing a man. I just hope Gervais breaks the chain but he's always fighting so I don't know. Sure got a bad beating this afternoon. From Mullu, he said."

"How did Mrs. Lafollette take it?" Mother asked.

"Well, when I went up to the house she and the kids were sitting at the kitchen table eating bread and meat. She had a scarf over her head and used the corner of it to wipe her eyes every so often but she wasn't carrying on like so many of these French women do when somebody's died. Lacotte, of course, had already broken the news to her. She kept saying over and over again, 'Raoul, he always say he was born to be hanged.' She told me he was very drunk, that they'd kicked him out of Higley's saloon and that he was probably going to the barn to get the bottle he always kept hidden there. I asked her if she'd seen the body yet and she said no, that none of them had been down to the barn. I told her not to. Lafollette wasn't fit for any wife or kids to see. Tongue hanging out, eyes bulging, and blood from his nose all over his face. Gruesome! I told her to wait until after the undertaker had fixed him up." Dad fell silent.

"I feel sorry for his wife and children," Mother said. "They've always been poor. What will they do now?"

"I asked her if she had any money," Dad answered. "She said there wasn't a penny in the house so I told her the Township would take care of the funeral expenses and I'd see that she got an order up at Flinn's store for groceries to tide them over. Got to find some work for Gervais though. Wonder if he's big enough to load pulp? Anyway, I left a ten dollar bill on the table for her."

They buried Raoul Lafollette two days later. Father Hassel, our village priest, refused to follow the many suggestions that Lafollette be put to rest in the Township cemetery rather than in the Catholic one. "Though the poor dark soul never came to confession in his whole life, he's still one of ours. Dig his grave in the west part. That's unconsecrated ground that's never known holy water." And Father Hassel said a low mass for him. Few besides the family attended.

The word went around that no one went to the burial except the graveyard diggers and the undertaker, Ed Stenrud, and that just as they put the cheap pine coffin in the hole Ed asked them if someone couldn't say something good about the deceased before they covered it. There was a long silence before one man spoke. "Well," he said, "they claim he was good at snaring rabbits."

One afternoon, a few days later, Father Hassel came to our house for his weekly game of chess. Or for the glass of whiskey Dad always had ready for him. The two men liked each other and it was a chance for good civilized conversation. They also liked to beat each other and the games were played intensely with the prize being one of Ed Stenrud's cigars. The undertaker always sent each of them a box every Christmas. "Ed's a good businessman," Dad said.

So I wasn't surprised when he asked me to go down to the ledge in the cellar and bring him three cigars. "One for the pot and two for the whiskey," he grinned as they sat down at the chessboard and arranged the pieces. I got a book and went over to the baywindow to read but Dad would have none of it. "You clear out, Cully. You know the rules. Go help your mother. Haul in some wood."

But after I carried in some wood for the kitchen stove, I tiptoed up the back stairs carefully avoiding that third creaking board from the top and quietly went into the front bedroom. Because there was a register in the middle of the floor, it was a good place to listen. I'd heard lots of interesting things through that grating.

At first it was mostly chess talk about gambits and the Queen's Knight to the Rooks fourth and other moves or strategies I didn't understand. Then Father Hassel, after a silence, asked Dad if he'd signed the death certificate for Lafollette yet.

"Yes. I put down as suicide-strangulation but I haven't mailed it out."

"You haven't? Well, I'll take that pawn, Doctor. And may I ask why haven't you." The priest's voice was elaborately casual.

"You've just made a mistake, there, Father. Check!"

"Maybe you did too, Doctor. Higley told me Raoul Lafollette was far too drunk to be able to climb that ladder and fix the noose and the chain-fall. Of course, he may have sobered up. Just the same though it couldn't have been more than an hour after they kicked him out of the saloon."

I heard Dad clear his throat before he spoke. "OK," he said, "if you want to trade bish   's all right with me. But Father, people don't bleed from the nose wher   are hung by the neck. And Raoul still had a bottle in his pocket with an i   of whiskey in it when I examined him."

"And a   n about to hang himself would have emptied it. Makes sense," the priest. re   ied. "Now why did you make that move, Doctor? You're up to somethir . Caveat! Caveat!" They were quiet for a time.

"Dad roke the silence. "Now that's an ingenious move, Father, but I'm not going to let you suck me in. Not like last time. I'll just counter by moving my Queen over here, sir. Did Higley also tell you that Nurmi had been to the saloon looking for Raoul and with blood in his eyes? A short time after Raoul started home?"

"Yes," said the priest. "He told me that. Higley didn't know why Nurmi was so mad but I do. His daughter's three months pregnant and she's hiding in the house of one of my parishoners. Do you think . . . . . ?"

50

"Can't tell about these Finns, Father. They can go really berserk. And Nurmi had an uncle who hung himself. A religious fanatic, he was. A Holy Roller. Now Father, you know you can't get that rook out of the corner."

"Oh, yes, I can. Just wait a minute. And while you're waiting, Doctor, there was another very angry man on the scene too. Lacotte! When we carried Raoul into the barn to lay him on the hay till Ed came with the hearse to get him, we saw the carcass of a young steer hanging from the rafter. All skinned out and with one hind quarter gone and the hide lying in a corner. Lacotte was furious though he tried to hide it. But I don't think he was surprised to see it. Just mad. Purple in the face."

"Hmm, I heard last week someone had stolen Lacotte's big bull calf just like they did last year. So you think then that . . . . .?" Dad's voice trailed off.

"I think I've got you, Doctor. Check!"

"Oh no, not yet you haven't. I'll just bring the bishop back to protect my king and I'll trade you my bishop for your queen any time. By the way, Father, did you find a billfold on the body? Higley said Raoul had a lot of money on him. Claimed he had got it by selling his rifle and also having been paid for working the jammer down at the loading dock. Any man who sells his rifle in this country could well be contemplating suicide."

"That's right," said the priest. "Deer meat and potatoes and make it through the winter. But maybe Raoul left his billfold in the house on the way to the barn."

Dad sounded scornful. "Fat chance of that," he said. "No matter how drunk he was, a man keeps the money. Besides when I went up to see his wife she said they didn't have a penny in the house. Now, Father, you're the one in trouble. Check!"

There was a long silence before Father Hassel spoke. "You wage psychological warfare, Doctor," he said. "I'm finding it hard to concentrate. If what you said is true, then why would his wife put ten dollars in the poorbox when I administered the low mass. I know she did because there wasn't anything in it beforehand and I checked it right after the service. And no one else went near it. You're right. I am in trouble, Doctor! Non amo te, medicus!"

"Check!" Dad's voice was triumphant. "I've got you on the run, Father. I gave her a ten dollar bill. Is that what she put in the poorbox?"

"No, it was two fives. So she must have been down at the barn and . . . . . ."

"Check again, Father," Dad said. "I suppose you also saw that Gervais had been beaten up pretty badly, and that his mother kept a scarf over her head. French women don't wear scarves indoors, do they Father? Unless they have good reason? Check! By the way, I also learned that Gervais lied too. Mullu, the kid who he said beat him up had been up to Ewen visiting his uncle that day. Why did they lie, Father? Maybe you can ask them that the next time they come to confession."

"Before you say 'checkmate,' Doctor, I'm surrendering. You win and here's one of Ed's cigars for your pleasure. I would appreciate, sir, just another small shot of that very good whiskey." They were quiet for a time. Then the priest spoke again.

"Well, Doctor," he said. "I must be going back to my supper and my ugly housekeeper. That was a very good, though somewhat complicated, game. I shall skin you next time, sir. But before I go, may I offer you a bit of Latin for your spiritual guidance: 'Si finis bonus est, totum bonum est.' Do you know what that means, Doctor?"

"Yes," said my dad. "It means all's well that ends well. I'll send out that death certificate tomorrow. Thank you, Father.

THE PRIVY

It was on Midsummer's Day that Leif Larsen decided to start building The Perfect Outhouse. Leif had been thinking about it for almost a year. Now that he was 75 and retired from building log cabins and saunas, he had to have something to do. Handling those big logs had gotten to be too much for him and besides he'd had his bellyfull of people who became impatient with his slowness and careful craftsmanship. They didn't understand that it took time to do a job right. People said that Leif Larsen was the best log butcher in the whole U.P. The term was not derogatory; it was high praise. Any man could put up a shack but only a few log butchers like Leif could build one that a man could be proud of all his day.

The old Norwegian had everything ready for his project. The fall before, after the sap was out of the trees, he had selected and cut the logs from a thick stand of white cedars in Beaver Dam Swamp. Ten feet long they were and with no taper to speak of, each had a butt diameter of seven inches. Only in a very thick swamp could you find such uniform cedars, a swamp where they had to grow straight and tall to see sun. After felling the trees, Leif had peeled off the bark with a draw-knife and now in the early summer sunshine they gleamed white. Next to the log pile was a stack of boards, fresh pine lumber with no knot holes, and beside this was a smaller pile of flat rocks that Leif had hauled all the way from the shore of Lake Tioga in his wheelbarrow. All was ready.

He got out the plans he had drawn to scale on sheets of shelf paper the winter before and studied them as he sat on the chopping block. Not that Leif needed to look at them for he could see vividly in his mind every bit of his intended masterpiece. Seven by six feet and seven feet tall it would be. Hardwood floor and shingled roof. A two holer. Leif had been undecided for a long time about the latter. All you really needed as you sat there on your throne in the warm summer sun, with the blue bottle flies buzzing around, was just one hole. Olga, his wife, would never be joining him as he did his duty. Too shy and besides they never had to go at the same time. So why two holes? Well, for one thing it was the custom. One hole for a man to crap in and the other for pee. If you used the same hole for both, then the front edge of it would get soggy from the drip. Besides, it was better to have that second hole for the wood ashes and water so you could stir them up with a long handled shovel and reach every corner of the pit. The ash lye would keep it smelling sweet. Leif wasn't going to have any stink in his perfect outhouse. No sir! So it would be a two holer. The best two holer in the whole U.P.

The first thing Leif did was to get some string and stakes and measure out the corners and the pit. Out of the house came Olga with her arms akimbo and her tongue working hard. "Leif! What you doing now? You no put outhouse there. That's no place so close to house. Put back by old one by woodpile." Leif's back stiffened.

"No," he said. "I put it here where everybody can see how I make it so good. Why hide?"

She pleaded with him in vain. She pointed out that it would be much nearer to the well than the old one was and that being closer to the house wouldn't save any snow shoveling in the winter because he'd have to keep the path to the woodpile open anyway. Why have to make two paths? She argued that there was always a big snow drift forming there in the winter. "You can't keep the path open there like you can the other one."

But as only a Swede is more stubborn than a Dutchman, and only a Norwegian more bullheaded than a Swede, Leif had his way. As he started digging the pit, Olga began to weep for the first time in their forty years of married life. "I tell you one thing, Leif, I no use your outhouse, no! I not going have everybody in valley seeing me go take crap there. No! I use old one."

"I bust old one down, Olga!"

"OK", I use slop jar!" Leif kept digging.

His wife had a point. The Larsen's house was built on a minor hill at the edge of our big one and it overlooked the entire valley. Like so many others, no shade trees blocked the view. Many have wondered why so many of the farm houses in the U.P. sit there starkly in clearings devoid of any trees. They simply don't understand our hunger for all the sun we can get and our hidden fear of the encroaching forest. Clear a piece of land and in ten years its edges will be full of little poplars and spruce. Ten years more and they will half cover the place. Olga was right. Not only from the road to Lake Tioga and the Copper Country, but also in plain view of all the houses in the valley, Leif's perfect outhouse would be clearly visible. He wanted it that way.

I will skip over most of Leif's labor for it took him all summer to complete his project. The work went slowly but careful. The logs had to be measured, cut to size, and then with axe, saw and chisel, fitted together so tightly that no caulking was needed. The ends were dovetailed and the bottom logs set upon a stone foundation. A box of cedar boards enclosed the pit so no dirt could fall in.

On the inside, each corner held a long cedar post thrust deeply into the ground so that even fifty kids couldn't dump it over on Halloween. An enclosed wood ventilator box ran upward from the pit to a screened opening under the eaves so there would be no smell or flies when you sat in place. Making the holes and hole covers alone took a week's work, cutting, beveling and sanding. When Leif tried to measure Olga's legs to make sure the holes would be just far enough from the floor she kicked him. It took half a day in the swamp to find just the right kind of cedar roots for a coat hanger and for the paper holder. No Sears catalog for this outhouse. Roll paper, the best!

The door gave Leif some trouble. After he had it put together and in place, it just didn't look right when it was open. Sort of spoiled the symmetry. So the old Norwegian built double doors like those on the church, each one with a long window in it so he could see out over the valley when he sat on this throne. That took care of that!

As you can imagine, once the news got around that Leif was building The Perfect Outhouse, he had a lot of company. All of us admired real craftsmanship and day after day one man or another would be up there on the hill watching him work or arguing religion. You see, Leif Larson was the town athiest, though he called himself a free thinker. He didn't believe in Heaven or Hell at all and he opined that maybe there was a God but he hadn't seen him yet. As for going to church, Leif didn't. He said that the first time he'd been there they threw water on him and the second time they saddled him with Olga and he supposed that the next time they'd take him out, put him in a hole and throw dirt in his face. He liked to argue, Leif did, and people used to egg him on to see what outrageous things he would say next.

After the roof was on and shingled, Leif walked down to the valley to take a look. No, it wasn't quite right. Pretty good but not perfect! The cedar logs were already getting gray from weathering. Should he varnish them? No, varnish always flaked off when it froze. So Leif used paint instead, bright yellow and white and blue, Norwegian colors, alternating on each log. Yah, that was better. Nobody could miss seeing it even though they were half a mile away. It sure stood out fine, there on the hill.

About the time Leif finished the painting, an old friend, Anders Lundberg, a Deacon in the Lutheran church, came up to pass the time of day and once again to try to make Leif see the error of his ways. "Nice job, Leif," he said admiringly, "but you not make outhouse; you make little church, yah. You religious down deep."

After Anders left, what he'd said troubled Leif and made him angry. "OK, they want church, I give them church!" And grinning a bit to himself at the sacrilege, he put a little steeple on top of the outhouse. And it did look better. It really did look like a tiny church on the hill when the doors were swung open.

Although he should have known what would happen, Leif was unprepared for the storm of protest that swept our town. Olga wouldn't speak to him, nor would his old friends - except to give him hell. "Take it off; take off that steeple or we will," they told him. You could almost feel the ostracism developing that our town always used when one of its folk had done the unforgivable deed.

Nevertheless, the next morning Leif went out to see his beautiful outhouse and use it for the first time. Everything was done and done right and it shone in the sun. But as he sat there on the fur lined hole, nothing would come. He pushed hard and harder but nothing. Three times that day he went back and tried again to no avail. It wasn't just that maybe he had really built a church. It was that he couldn't bring himself to pollute perfection.

That evening Leif drank a bottle of whiskey, soaked his outhouse with kerosene and burned it down.

THE BALLOON

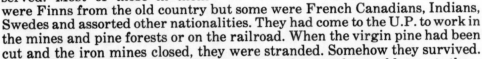

My father, Dr. John Gage, was the only physician in a large wilderness area. Tioga with its six hundred so-called souls was its largest town but there were several scattered hamlets and many isolated cabins or homestead farms that he served. Most of those in them were Finns from the old country but some were French Canadians, Indians, Swedes and assorted other nationalities. They had come to the U.P. to work in the mines and pine forests or on the railroad. When the virgin pine had been cut and the iron mines closed, they were stranded. Somehow they survived.

They liked and respected my father not only because he would come to them day or night, whether or not they could pay for his services, but because he was tough and fearless, the ultimate virtues in that rough land. They had heard how, when all the others had fled, Dr. Gage had gone to an isolated lumber camp full of smallpox and had stayed there three days and nights, tending the sick and dying. (Dad hated smallpox with a passion. He never could stand the smell of burnt sugar because he said it was just like the odor of a man dying from smallpox.) And they knew how their doctor, with Jim Johnson, the deputy sheriff, had put on their old clothes walked up the Northwestern Railroad track to meet an armed murderer who had escaped from the prison at Marquette. Pretending to be section hands and carrying only a pick and a shovel, they had captured the escapee and brought him back in handcuffs.

Our people also remembered how when Maggi O'Rourke went insane and was screaming and cursing and waving a butcher knife threatening to cut the little doctor's throat if he came near, Dad had calmly walked to the door and said, "Maggie, if those people are bothering you. I'll send them away and then give you something so you can sleep." That same knife was in our kitchen cabinet when I was a boy and it was indeed very sharp.

Yet my father had one real fear. It was of fire, house fires or forest fires, especially. He'd seen too many horribly burned men, women and children trapped inside their one door cabins when the stove pipes, too full of creosote, had caught fire and exploded in the middle of the night. And he had seen the terrible holocaust of a crown fire racing fast along the tops of pitch-filled jackpines. Dad loved the forest and the desolate aftermath of a big burn always affected him deeply. Once he took me trout fishing on Blaney Creek and pointed to a large area of charred snags. "See those, Cully. Two years ago they were young white pines, all about fifteen feet tall. I think I know who did it too. La Seur! That old French devil sets forest fires each year on these plains just so he can have better blueberries. Hope he doesn't get sick."

Everywhere Dad went in the woods, he put up *Prevent Forest Fire* signs. You could almost know where he went fishing or partridge hunting. He gave talks to the school kids and got a conservation man from Down Below to train a selected group of men in fighting forest fires. As Township Supervisor, he arranged to have shovels, axes and pails stored in our little tin covered firehouse in the event that a forest fire might threaten the town. Even at home, Dad never discarded the match with which he had lit his pipe without making sure it was out and then breaking it in two to be sure. Sometimes even in the middle of winter when it was way below zero, he'd let the house fires go out in the stoves and clean the stove pipes of their soot and creosote. Yes, he was scared of fires.

I started this tale planning to tell you how we celebrated the Fourth of July in Tioga early in this century and I guess I got to talking so much about my father because he played an important part in the experience. Every year he got a big wooden box full of assorted fireworks and put on quite a show once it got dark and the townspeople and their kids lined up along our picket fence to watch the display.

The Fourth of July I remember best was in 1914 when I was nine years old. It began when the sun came up over the valley and the church bells rang and every shotgun in town went boom. Then came the sporadic rattle of firecrackers as the kids went into action. They had saved the money they got from selling arbutus to the passengers or trainmen on the Milwaukee and St. Paul Railroad; they had stashed away every cent they'd received for doing errands or odd chores. And they had blown all of it at Flinn's store on cap pistols and rolls of caps, or torpedoes, snakes, but especially on firecrackers.

The latter came in assorted sizes from the big four inchers called yellow jackets to packages of very tiny ones whose fuses were so intertangled that most of us just set fire to the whole package at once and revelled in the banging and crackling that resulted. Always there were some that were duds and these we touched off individually. If they had no fuses, we bent them in half, made a cut on the bend, and then they'd go off without a bang but with a satisfactory whoosh. We called them squibs.

The standard sized red firecrackers were about an inch and a half long and made a good loud bang when we touched them to the burning brown punk. Gad, that was fun! Even toddlers barely able to walk were provided with a spool on the end of a long stick into which a firecracker was inserted and lit by their parents. Some of the girls used the sticks and spools too, screeching when the explosion came, but not us boys. That was sissy stuff. Often we'd light a cracker and throw it into the air, but usually we lit it on the ground or a crack in the sidewalk or porch. If we had been wealthy enough to buy a three incher, we'd hide it under a tin can with just the fuse sticking out and enjoy seeing how high the can would be shot into the air. Or we'd pretend to be iron ore miners and put a larger firecracker into the side of a sandbank to see how big a hole we could blast. Sometimes we'd join the fuses of four or five firecrackers together, light them and run.

The torpedoes, little balls of powder covered with paper and having a cap inside, we'd have to throw hard on a rock before they exploded and often they didn't but wow, were they loud! Made your ears ring. The snakes were for sissies. You'd light a little white tube and it would elongate, twisting along the ground as it grew. Then if you touched it afterwards, it would collapse into ashes. We called them "snakes in the grass." Some of us also bought a few "son-of-a-guns." These were round circles of explosives about as big as a quarter. We put them on a flat rock, then ground them under our heels. This set off spurts of crackling fire in every direction. Only the kids who had shoes, and not many of us did in summer, tried these son-of-a-guns or spit devils.

By ten o'clock in the morning, the hound dogs could come out from under the barns where they'd been hiding, for most of the ammunition had been shot off. Only a few intermittent bangs could be heard as the kids salvaged a firecracker or two. It was then that Dad set off some of the giant firecrackers he'd got in the box of fireworks. They were huge red things, about ten inches tall and two inches in diameter with a square wood base. Dad would light the long fuse then run and hide behind a clump of maple trees. What an explosion! The biggest boom in the world! Kids from all over town would come running to see him shoot off another. The only thing comparable was when Ed Stenrud, our undertaker, once put a half stick of dynamite under his garbage pile and blew it to hell and high water. By noon the town was quiet again.

In the afternoon all the townspeople and their kids traipsed down to the beach at Lake Tioga about a mile away. There they heard speakers patriotically praising our country and its ideals, and heard our makeshift band play the Star Spangled Banner and My Country Tis of Thee. A Spanish War veteran told of his war experiences in Cuba in a faltering voice that no one heard clearly; American flags waved everywhere.

Then we watched the birling matches in which two lumberjacks got on a big pine log and began rotating it with their spiked boots. By stopping suddenly, one of them tried to dump the other one into the lake. Next came the drilling matches. A huge granite boulder was attacked by three-men drilling teams of miners. Two of them with huge fifty pound sledges hammered the long drill while the third turned the drill bit after every tenth slam. Clang, turn, clang! Which team could get the drill down into the rock all the way to its white band first? It was exciting and we always wondered what would happen if the sledgers missed. Finally, there was the greased pig let loose for anyone to catch and take home. Great hilarity!

But the best was yet to come - my father's fireworks. To us kids it seemed as though it would never get dark enough to start them but finally about the time the moon came up, Dad set off the pinwheels on the pillars of our porch. Every inch of space along our picket fence was occupied by people or kids, sometimes three deep. Then came the Roman candles. How proud I was when I was old enough to wave one in a circle and shoot the red, yellow and green balls of fire high into the air. Next came the skyrockets, placed carefully in their troughs, and trailing sparks to great heights over the schoolyard before they exploded and discharged their display of colored lights. "Oooooh!" yelled the crowd.

Red flares were then set alight and in their glow my father soaked tight balls of shredded excelsior in kerosene. Now was the moment of moments - the fire balloons. Holding the tissue paper upright, Dad lit the excelsior in the ring below it. Ah, too bad! The damned thing caught fire and burned right there on the ground. He tried again with the second balloon and the same thing happened. One big flare and the balloon was ashes. The crowd groaned with disappointment. There was only one more. But this one did not burn. It swelled until its five foot length was filled and slowly it rose as the people cheered. Up, up it went and then catching the breeze at about a hundred feet, it floated east down the street with many of the screaming kids following it. Finally they lost sight of it over the dark trees where the old stage coach trail to the Copper Country used to run.

Dad then passed out sparklers to all the kids still at the fence and after a bit we went to bed. It had been a fine unsafe and unsane Fourth of July.

The only trouble was that next morning we awoke choking with wood smoke. The worst forest fire we'd ever had was roaring east of town. Probably began where Dad's balloon came down. Anyway, it was called Doctor's Fire from then on.

THE CROW THAT TALKED

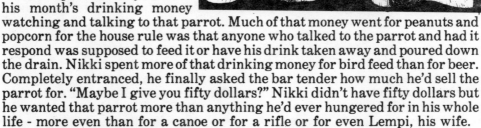

I t was in a bar in Hancock that Nikki Sippola first fell in love with a bird. It was a yellow and green parrot, a nasty dispositioned but lovely critter who when it felt like it would say "No crackers!" or "Who the hell are you?" or "What? What?" as well as some other profane and vivid expressions taught to him by the customers. One of its sayings, which I can mention because it was spoken in Finnish, was "Saatana pelikeda - buscan housu." Nikki never told us kids what it meant but he laughed every time he spoke of it, so it must have been choice. Nikki spent two days and all his month's drinking money watching and talking to that parrot. Much of that money went for peanuts and popcorn for the house rule was that anyone who talked to the parrot and had it respond was supposed to feed it or have his drink taken away and poured down the drain. Nikki spent more of that drinking money for bird feed than for beer. Completely entranced, he finally asked the bar tender how much he'd sell the parrot for. "Maybe I give you fifty dollars?" Nikki didn't have fifty dollars but he wanted that parrot more than anything he'd ever hungered for in his whole life - more even than for a canoe or for a rifle or for even Lempi, his wife.

The bartender laughed. "For fifty dollars you might get a canary. I wouldn't take five thousand for the bird. It brings in more trade than anything I could do. Made fifty dollars on peanuts alone last month. The parrot eats some and the customers eat some and then they get thirsty and have to drink more beer. Fifty dollars? You're crazy, man!"

Noticing how disappointed Nikki looked, the bartender said, "Why don't you get a young crow and teach it to talk? I seen one once up at Hibbing who was pretty good though not like old Bill here. It could say, "What? What? What?"and "Dammit!" and some other things. Fact is, that's what give me the idea to buy this parrot. I hear though that crows are harder to teach than parrots and that you got to get them young, just before they leave the nest."

"I can get a young crow I think," said Nikki, "but even if I did, how'd I go about learning him to talk?"

"I dunno for sure," answered the bartender. "Old Bill here was talking when I got him but he's learned most of his dirty words at the bar. You just got to catch him when he's about ready to talk and then say something simple over and over. And if he does say something even if it's not just quite right, you give him something to eat. But he's got to be hungry. I don't know what crows eat."

"Hell, they'll eat anything," said Nikki, "specially if it's rotten. Corn for sure and maybe worms or bits of rotten meat. That's no trouble." He was getting enthusiastic.

"Well, let me know how you come out," grinned the bartender. "I may need a spare bird if old Bill gets sick or dies. And I'll pay you fifty bucks for your crow if he can talk."

"No, you don't!" Nikki replied. "Five thousand, mebbe!"

By the time spring came and the crows returned, Nikki had his cage ready. It had taken many hours of gathering and peeling straight willow shoots, then nailing them onto the frame of a box four by four by four feet. A crow needed a big cage, not enough to fly in of course, but large enough to get around in. Then there had to be a door and a substantial perch where the crow could sit while Nikki taught it to talk. And a feed pan and water can.

"Why you no wait till you catch your crow?" asked his wife Lempi. She was highly dubious about the entire project. "You not going to keep that cage in my house. Out in the barn maybe OK." Lempi kept the cleanest house in town. A perfectionist. People opined that maybe she was that way because she'd never been able to have children, a great sorrow to both her and her husband. Indeed one of the reasons Nikki was so interested in having a talking bird was that it would bring kids to the place. Nikki always liked to have us around and Lempi often brought out a cinnamon roll when we dropped by. But we had to eat it outside and not bring any dirt into her spotless kitchen. She was a cleaner, Lempi was. Why she scrubbed her floors with lye water sometimes three times a week and Nikki had to leave his boots on the porch or, if it were snowing, on a rug in the summer kitchen before entering the house. There'd be no dirty bird in her house.

The crows returned the tenth of April that year and Nikki spent a lot of time in the woods locating where they went to roost at night and studying their habits. He also practiced calling them. He'd always had the gift. You just had to squeeze your neck muscles and make a sound like clearing your throat only louder to make a good caw. But now he learned that there were a lot of different kinds of cawings. Three short sharp caws meant danger; it was a warning to all the other crows. One single long caw meant that everything was all right. Two caws, the last with an upward rise in pitch, seemed to mean that the crow had found something interesting and was inviting other crows to join it. But there were other sounds as well, especially after they had gone to roost: little gurglings, cooings, and even some sounds like those made by a human baby. Nikki practiced imitating all of them. "Maybe I've got to learn crow talk first," he thought. "Maybe if I imitate the mother of the crow I'm going to get, it may imitate me and then I can start teaching him."

About the middle of May the crows began flying eratically, the males pursuing the females all over the skies. They'd suddenly rise, then plunge downwards. From his blind, Nikki watched their courtship. One bird actually turned a somersault after soaring abruptly, then falling. On the tree limbs or occasionally on the forest floor, he watched the males spread their black tails, curve their necks and strut along with their wings drooping. No cawing then, more cooing than anything else. The female was less active but finally she would begin to respond when he came close to her, touching her bill to his, and fluttering her wings. Often two or three other crows would sit above the love pair on a branch watching the show and giving the two-caw call that meant there was something good going on. Quite a performance!

Shortly after the mating, the birds began their nests. Nothing fancy, and mainly assembled from branches and twigs and grass, they seemed almost thrown together in the crotch of a branch high up in a large pine or maple tree. Almost the size of a squirrel's nest. Somehow, Nikki was able to locate four nests altogether but two of them were over four miles from town on the south shore of Lake Tioga. The closest one was back of Mount Baldy and it was in a medium size maple that looked climbable once you got to the first branch about twenty feet up. Moreover it had a limb parallel but lower than the one holding the nest so Nikki felt he could slide along it to see what was inside or to get the fledgling.

He built a good blind nearby and dragged an old ladder out to the tree one night shortly after the nest was completed, then blazed a trail so he could find the tree in the dark if he used his miner's carbide head lamp. He didn't much relish climbing up there in the darkness and wouldn't do it unless he had to but he had to get that young crow.

Once Nikki saw that the female was sitting on the nest he kept away from the area for more than a month fearing that he might disturb the hatching. Then, when he did return, he went to the blind before dawn to watch the young birds being fed. So far as he could tell there were only three of them, one larger than the others. "He's the one for me," said Nikki.

Finally after long waiting he saw one of the little crows stand up and walk a few feet out on the limb before returning to the nest. It was time! When Nikki began to climb the ladder what a torrent of cawing arose. Crows from everywhere seemed to swoop around him. One grabbed his cap and dropped it to the ground. Another clawed his face as it swooped by. So that night, Nikki put on his headlight and climbed the tree and got his crow, the biggest one in the nest. It didn't protest; just huddled in his hand as he put it in the bag and when he opened the cage door back in the barn and set it in a sort of a nest he'd prepared in a corner, the crow promptly went to sleep. Wasn't hurt a bit.

The next morning Nikki looked it over. The little crow was about six or seven inches long and not quite feathered out. And it was hungry. Its beak seemed almost bigger than its head and it squawked as Nikki fed it bits of worms and little balls of corn meal mush. Nikki imitated the sqawking and tried to give the bird its food only after it made some kind of sound. By the end of the week he could hold the crow as he fed it. You could almost see it grow.

Nikki named the little crow Akkari (Oscar) after his brother-in-law although Lempi's brother was dumb and Akkari was bright. Indeed it was a quick learner. Nikki only had to dip its beak in the water pan once to teach it to drink and by the end of the first month it would answer back when Nikki made some cooing or cawing but only if it was hungry. That was no problem because at first the little crow was always famished. It would eat almost anything Nikki put before him: peas, berries, household scraps, chickenfeed, but it preferred meat scraps or worms. After every rain Nikki picked nightcrawlers in the garden for Akkari.

By the end of August the crow was full grown and had acquired a few words. Nikki had tried at first to teach it the Finnish word "Mitta?" but that failed so he settled for its English equivalent "What?" which more or less resembled a caw. Akkari picked that up fast. For a time, whenever Nikki said anything, the bird would ask "What? What?" It really sounded like it wanted to know. Akkari sure got some bits of nightcrawler when he first said it.

The next word the bird learned was "Hello!" perhaps because all of us kids used to say it so often when we'd visit the Sippolas. It wasn't quite right, being more like "Allo!" but it was clear enough. The bird's first sentence was "I come back" - again perhaps because Nikki and all of us said it to the crow when we'd leave him and give him food to carry him over. It sounded a bit slurred but you could understand it all right. Akkari also learned some other words and phrases that I forget but what I remember most vividly was his laughter. First, he'd give a shrill whistle and then say, "Ha! . . .Ha, ha, ha, ha!" It almost sounded human and anyone who heard it couldn't help laughing in return.

Anyone, that is, except Lempi. Nikki's wife couldn't abide that crow even if it was in the barn. She was jealous of the long hours her husband spent with the bird. "You getting so you don't talk anyone else!" she complained. Besides, she was appalled at the bird's dirtiness. Nikki did his best to keep the cage clean, putting fresh burlap bags on the floor every day and washing them in the creek behind the house. He was always glad when I brought him some of our old newspapers for the same purpose. But Lempi was right. Crows are almost as bad as geese. What goes in one end usually comes out of the other and soon the barn was smelling pretty high. "And you, too, Nikki," said his wife. "You start smelling like crow too. You wash again." Nikki took a lot of saunas during those months.

The Sippolas had a big fight when fall came and the nights got cold. Nikki wanted to bring the cage into the house but Lempi was so angry all the time he didn't even bring it up. Instead, at first snowfall, he brought the cage into the summer kitchen and had it out with Lempi. Oh, how she raged and raged. Oh how she argued! Nikki tried to explain that he was making money, big raha, that in the spring when the bird had learned a few more words and especially to say, "Akkari wants peanuts!" he would sell it to some bar owner for "thousands of dollars, Lempi!" She was not convinced. "Sometime I wring its neck like chicken!"

"You do that and I bust you in nose good!" he answered. "We keep Akkari over winter in summer kitchen, not in house."

And that's the way it was. Nikki had his way for once but it was a hard winter. The summer kitchen, a shed off the real kitchen, was usually never heated in the winter. It was used only on the hot days of summer for cooking, baking and heating the wash water in the copper boiler. Many of our houses had summer kitchens; they kept our houses cool, but in the winter they were only for hanging up bacon, deer carcasses or smoked fish. No one built a fire in the summer kitchen's range during the snow months.

But Nikki did and it came hard at times to wake himself up two or three times at night to fire up the stove again so his crow would stay warm enough. And, as you can imagine, he had to work pretty hard to keep the smell down. Lempi never entered the room without holding her nose and all in all she made Nikki's life pretty miserable that winter.

It was in the middle of April when Nikki got up very early one morning to go netting trout in Goose Lake. There was still a big sheet of ice in the middle but a ring of open water could be seen along the shore. By setting an illegal gill net in the shallows of this ring, you could usually come back with a sack full of trout. But you had to get up before dawn, before the game warden did. Nikki arose and dressed, ate a bit, and then cleaned out the crow's cage, put clean newspapers down, and was on his way.

Unfortunately, he didn't close the cage door tight enough. When he returned that noon Akkari was strutting around the table cloth on the kitchen table and Lempi was gone. She did leave a note: "No more! I go my sister's house in Marquette and I no come back so long you have that dirty bird."

Nikki was deeply hurt by her leaving but he was also defiant. "OK, if she go, she go. I make it OK." He brought the cage into the kitchen and put it by the window on Lempi's chair. Cooking wasn't so bad though he got awful tired of bacon and eggs and liver sausage. No homemade bread. No cinnamon rolls. No pie. No dinner pail all fixed when he went to work.

And somehow, everything got pretty dirty. Nikki would sweep the floors and try to put things away but the dishes piled up. Washing his clothes was a terrible chore and they never really got clean. Why, he didn't have any time to do anything but take care of the house and that damned bird. Moreover Akkari hadn't learned any new sayings except "Shut up!" Nikki had tried his utmost to get the crow to say "More peanuts" to increase his salability but all he got were the same old words or that damned whistle and laugh. Maybe that's why it learned "Shut up!" Nikki would say it so often. Lonesome and troubled, sometimes Nikki almost hated that damned bird.

It wasn't till the middle of July that Nikki decided that living alone wasn't worth it so he went down to Higley's saloon and offered to sell Akkari. He told Higley how much trade the parrot had brought into the bar in Hancock and how it would liven up the place. Higley just laughed. "How much you want for that damned crow?" he asked.

Nikki started at a thousand dollars and ended up offering the bird for fifty. Higley just laughed some more. "Nikki," he said finally, "I wouldn't take that damned crow of yours if you gave it away. I got enough dirty birds at the bar every night as it is. No!"

Because it was impossible to get away and go to Hancock just then, or to Ishpeming or Marquette, Nikki found a farmer up beyond the old furnace who would care for the crow free. Besides, the man had a kid who had often come to see and talk to Akkari like the rest of us did. So Nikki, feeling bad, took the cage and the crow to its new but temporary home. In the fall Nikki would take the bird up to the Copper Country or somewhere and get a bunch of money. Meanwhile he could at least visit it once in a while.

The house sure seemed empty with both Akkari and Lempi gone. Nobody to talk to. Not much to do. So finally Nikki wrote Lempi, asking her to come back. This is what he wrote. "Dear Lempi: You win. I get rid of Akkari. You no see him again. Come home." He even signed it "Love, Nikki."

Lempi came up on the afternoon train next day and the whole town was glad. "I lonesome for you too, Nikki," she said as she hugged him. Although he had cleaned the house very hard, she did it all over, happily. And she baked him bread and cinnamon rolls, even a blueberry pie. It was like old times -very good. And it was very good to hold her in his arms that night with a cool wind blowing in through the open window. Nikki slept better than he had for months.

Until shortly after dawn, when Lempi shook him and pointed to the window. There on the sill was Akkari. "I come back," the crow said. "Hello, Hello!" And then it gave the shrill whistle and laughed.

Nikki pulled the covers back over his head.

A BOY AND HIS HORSE

H alf the people in town were down at the depot that afternoon in the summer of 1913 when the salesman from Green Bay drove my father's newly purchased Model-T Ford out of the boxcar and off the ramp. It was the first automobile most of them had ever seen and they ooh-ed and ah-ed when the motor started. The salesman was there to give Dad directions for cranking it ("always keep your thumb tucked in or you'll break your arm!"), for setting the spark and throttle levers on the steering wheel, and for using the clutch and brake pedals. "Let the clutch out easy, Doc," he advised, "or it'll stall or jerk like an unbroken broncho. It's a knack."

After demonstrating the complicated process several times, he had my father try it. Then finally up the hill street they came, a rabble of yelling kids streaming behind. I'd never seen my father so proudly triumphant. When my mother came out to observe the glorious vehicle with its shiny brass radiator, wood-spoked wheels, and leather straps tied to the headlights, Dad almost burst with the glory of it. "No more damned horses, Edyth," he said still shaking from the vibration. "They say this shebang can even go thirty miles an hour. Why I can make calls in half the time."

Dad had some trouble learning to drive but he kept at it. Whenever he put on the brakes, he also pulled back on the steering wheel as though it were reins, sometimes even roaring "Whoa!" Possessed of little mechanical aptitude, he often gave the engine too much spark or too little throttle and so getting the Ford started usually took a good ten minutes. He even had difficulty putting the top up and the isinglass curtains in place when it rained. Those early tires were always getting punctured or suffering blow-outs which meant jacking up the axle, taking the tire off the wheel and vulcanizing and patching it right there. No spare. It was a most complicated procedure for my father and he almost wore out the Owner's Manual reading and rereading it.

But how proud and delighted he was to take us out for a drive even though it was usually just up and down our street. There were no gravel roads then, just wagon ruts outside our village limits. Dad navigated them when he had to but they were not for pride or pleasure. When she went with him, mother would put on her brown duster robe and fasten a veil over her hat with long hatpins. When we met a horse and wagon, Dad would squeeze the rubber bulb on the horn as a warning, then come to a complete stop to let the rig by. Horses were terrified of the sight, sound and smell of the first automobile. Often when my father parked it outside our house, farmers would drive up their teams to have their horses smell it. Then they'd ask Dad to start the engine while they held their shying nags tightly. They didn't want any runaways when later they met us on the road.

At that time there were no garages or filling stations anywhere in the whole U.P. Dad would have a barrel of gasoline sent up on the train and this would then be hauled to our barnyard to be set up against a bank. To fill the car tank, we'd first have to strain the gasoline through chamois cloth into the pour can and we had to make sure that the wheel cups were always full of axle grease.

Dad also had to be his own service man even unto grinding the valves. When major repairs were needed such as overhauling the engine, he usually got an old Cousin Jack (Cornish) miner who had repaired the big machinery in the mine's engine house. They'd put a chain hoist onto a big limb of a maple tree and lift the engine out of the car so they could work on it. Sometimes the town blacksmith had to make a new part. All in all, owning a car in 1913 was no small deal.

Despite the envy of my friends, I hated that automobile with a passion. Indeed, my father almost had to force me to ride in it. At first he thought it was because I was scared of the noise and speed but I wouldn't even sit in it when it was silent and unmoving. Then he thought it was bcause I was sick and he gave me calomel and castor oil. Only after some weeks did he discover that my reluctance came because I was afraid he would sell Billy, the horse I loved so dearly. He did sell Prince, our other horse, almost immediately and I was glad of that. A mean critter, a kicker and a biter. Once that black devil cornered me in the box stall and I had to flatten myself along the wall under the long feedbox so he couldn't get to me - a long and terrible half hour. Until Dad bought the Ford he always kept two horses and kept both of them tired out, making his house calls all over the countryside, summer and winter no matter what the weather.

Oh how relieved I was when he told me he wouldn't sell Billy, that he needed him when the car broke down (which was frequently) and also that he would have to have some means of transportation during the spring break-up when the dirt roads becme impassible.

To Dad, Billy was the spare horse and he had originally bought him both for that purpose but also becuse he wanted my mother to have a horse she could ride. My mother was a gentlewoman, city reared, who in her youth had done a lot of riding, side saddle of course. I used to love to see her on Billy, with that little derby pinned to her brown hair, galloping down to Lake Tioga and back on a fine summer's day. She rode him well. By the time I began to ride Billy however, arthritis had set in and she no longer could do it. But she encouraged me and bought me a real western saddle with a horn on it that I could hang onto while learning to ride. By the time I was twelve I was galloping everywhere with confidence and ease.

Let me tell you a bit about Billy. A pure white gelding, he was not a big horse, as horses go. Dad said that he had raced in his early years and I believe it because he could never resist turning on a burst of speed automatically whenever anything went past him - even a train. Billy could jump too. I'll never forget how he took off over a big log that had fallen across one of the old logging roads - so smooth and easy - and then how he looked at me over his shoulder as if to say, "Nothing to it!"

Most horses are pretty dumb but Billy wasn't. In fact, he almost seemed to have a sense of humor enjoying the little tricks he played on me. Always when I put on the saddle blanket and then the saddle and started to tighten the cinch straps, he'd swell up his belly thereby insuring that the saddle would slip and dump me off when I got on. Then he'd whinny in delight. I swear that when I first took him down to the lake to have a drink and he went down on his knees while I went over his head into the water, he grinned and whinnied almost a horse laugh! Again and again when I tried to put on his bridle in the winter months, Billy would play a game with me, clenching his huge teeth tightly so I couldn't insert the cold bit. Not that it was too cold either for I always warmed it first by putting it inside my shirt but I'd always have to sweet talk him, stroke, currycomb or brush him all over before he'd open his mouth. Yet once, when I foolishly galloped him across the railroad tracks down by the depot and he caught a hoof in the rails and fell upon me breaking my leg in two places, Billy stood there until help came. He stood over me with one foot in the air, fearing to put it down lest he'd step on me.

How I loved that white horse! Not just riding him along the forest trails but also caring for him. Never did it seem like chorework; it was always a labor of love. Climbing up into the loft and throwing down the fragrant hay that still held the smell of summer in it, scooping out a more than generous helping of oats from the bin (and being careful not to have a mouse in the bucket), I'd watch him eat with great pleasure. I always warmed his water in the winter. Even cleaning out the stable was a privilege, not a duty, and now in my old age when I use horse manure to make the compost I need to attempt to grow *The Perfect Potato*, I think of Billy. Always I had fresh straw for him and I brushed and currycombed him until he shone. When I brought him a carrot or apple from the house, he'd nibble it daintily from my hand and nuzzle my pockets to see if I'd brought along a sugar lump, the long kind that the old Finn women used to suck their coffee through from the saucer.

And I talked to him, sharing my hurts and hopes and dreams.

Finally it became apparent that Billy was growing very old. It was painful to see him trying to get up on his feet in the morning. His nose was getting grey. I couldn't bear to urge him to gallop anymore for he tired so swiftly. Sometimes I'd get down and lead him rather than ride the forest trails. Billy didn't eat as much and he ate very slowly. There also seemed to be a film over his eyes, and he became lame. No longer when I'd go down to the pasture to call him would he come charging up to me at the fence shinnying. Instead, I'd have to go to him and pat and stroke his sides before he seemed to recognize me enough to follow me back to the barnyard or stable. It was heart breaking to see my friend plodding heavily and painfully up the lane.

Then one morning I overheard my father telling my mother that he'd have to do something about old Billy. "He's no use to us and Cully doesn't even ride him anymore. Maybe I'd better shoot him to put him out of his miseries. Or perhaps I could get someone to lead him down to the slaughter house and have them take care of it." My mother protested, saying that I would never forgive him if he did such a thing, that it would be better just to leave Billy in the pasture until he died. Dad just grunted and I remembered how once when I was very young, he made me wallop against a sapling a wounded rabbit he'd shot - until it died. "I want to teach you, Cully, that it's not unkind to put an end to suffering," he'd said when I weepingly obeyed him.

Watching Billy in his last days was a bad time. The bottom seemed to have dropped out of my world. I couldn't eat, and it was hard to sleep. One moonlight night I crept out of my bed and walked down to the pasture to see if old Billy was all right, then slept in the grass beside him until dawn came.

Dad didn't have to shoot Billy nor was he taken to the slaughter house to be sledged between the eyes and have his throat cut. One night we had one of our terrible U.P. thunderstorms with almost continuous flashes of zigzag lightening and rolling crashes of unbelievably loud thunder reverberating over our granite hills. The next morning I found Billy dead in the pasture. With burn streaks going down his mane to his legs, he had been killed instantly by lightening.

66

I dug his grave myself, nine feet by six, and five feet deep, an undertaking that took most of the day. Then I rounded up some of the kids who too had ridden him and with great effort we finally managed to put him into the huge hole. Then I sent them away and covered Billy with all the flowers I could find in the pasture, mainly daisies and Indian Paint Brush, and shoveled the earth over him, weeping so hard I could hardly see.

Sixty some years later, I still ache, remembering.

THE WAKE

uring the winter months there wasn't much for a man to do in the evenings except to go to bed - which is why there were so many kids in Tioga. Oh, you could grease your shoepacs, put a new handle on the axe, boil your

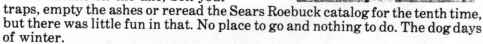

traps, empty the ashes or reread the Sears Roebuck catalog for the tenth time, but there was little fun in that. No place to go and nothing to do. The dog days of winter.

Nevertheless, there were five men in our town who had found a way to get away from their wives and children once a week on Saturday night. They had a sort of club, the Last Man Under the Table Club, which met in the back room of Callahan's store to play poker and empty a keg of beer.

It wasn't much of a store that the Mike and Dinny Callahan brothers operated. Little on the shelves except pork and beans and other staples. No meats. Just coffee, sugar, Peerless smoking tobacco and Red Man snuff; boxes of dried prunes, apples and apricots; a barrel of crackers and a big wheel of yellow cheese made up most of the inventory. But Callahans' stayed open until nine at night every day of the week, and being located next to the post office it attracted enough business to keep the two bachelor Irishmen afloat.

Behind the main part of the store was the room where the Last Man Under the Table Club had its fun, and behind this was a smaller room where Ed Stenrud, our undertaker, kept his coffins and caskets and did his dirty work. Sort of a spooky place but it was alive and full of hilarity when the five regulars slapped down their cards, made their bets and drank till they were thoroughly polluted.

They were a motley crew, those regulars. First there was Dinny Callahan, the store keeper, who had started the club some years before. So long as Dinny was half sober, he kept the sessions lively with his thick Irish brogue, laughter and song. But he was one of those unfortunate souls who couldn't hold his liquor very well. Four mugs of beer and perhaps a shot of whiskey and Dinny's eyes would begin to glaze; five mugs and he would slowly slide off his chair and pass out. Dinny was always the first man under the table. Didn't make any difference. The others, without a glance, always played on. Occasionally, after half an hour or so, Dinny would revive enough to enter the game again but one more mug and he was blotto till morning.

The other four players were Laf Bodine, the red headed trapper we called King of the Poachers; Paddy Feeney, our blacksmith; Bill Maler, logger who had a homestead down by Lake Tioga; and Untu Salmonen, a big Finn who pumped the handcar up and down the railroad tracks maintaining the right-of-way. To all of them, these weekly poker sessions were the highlight of their lives.

They played straight draw-poker with deuces wild. Paddy, the blacksmith, was the banker and with five white chips or one red chip for a nickel and a blue chip for a dime, no one ever lost or won very much but they had a high old time. Actually, the game was just an excuse for getting thoroughly drunk, the traditional U.P. Saturday night spree. One keg of beer and perhaps a bottle of rotgut whiskey from Higley's saloon was usually enough to do the job. If they had hangovers the next morning, well that was the price you had to pay. You ought to get drunk on Saturday night.

But all good things come to an end and after seven years the *Last Man Under the Table Club* died a sudden death. Here's how it came about. The last session was much like all of those that had occurred before, but perhaps just a little louder and gayer because there were two bottles of rotgut instead of one to go with the keg. Laf, filling a long shot inside straight, warwhooped and pounded on the table. Untu with only a pair of threes and his six bet bluff was called by Bill Maler holding only a pair of nines, so he did a war dance around the big table, yelling with triumph. Dinny, the storekeeper, kept losing steadily as usual and kept drinking more and more so he could bear the taunts of the others. "Here's to the Irish! They always lose! Have another snort, Dinny!" Paddy wouldn't drink to that but instead started singing a sad song or two in honor of the ould sod.

It was about midnight when Dinny passed out and slid under the table. The other four played on, wondering who'd be the next to join him. Then Bill had a great idea. "Let's give Dinny an Irish wake," he proposed. "Let's get one of Ed Stenrud's coffins out of the back room and put Dinny in it until he sobers up." A burst of laughter greeted the suggestion and the deed was done. They didn't use one of Ed's fancy caskets but settled for the pine box Ed used for poor folk. Putting it on the floor beside the card table they continued their game, each one putting a blue chip in the pot for Dinny and taking a snort for him too. Finally, realizing that they were all getting shaky and wanting to see what Dinny would do when he came to, they stopped drinking and began putting on a mock wake. "Ah, Dinny was a fine man but he couldn't handle likker. It just made him sicker!" Great guffawing and pounding of knees! Someone got a candle from the back room, lit it and put it near the coffin. Laf played preacher and gave forth with a long sloppy sermon about our dear departed. More laughter, more suspense, more snorts. When would the bugger wake up?

Laf's talking of Kingdom Come reminded them of Sammy Hall, the old drinking song, and all joined in tipsily.

> "Oh, my name is Sammy Hall, Sammy Hall, Sammy Hall,
>   Oh my name is Sammy Hall and I hate you one and all,
> You're a gang of muckers all. Damn yer hides!
>
> Oh I killed a man, tis said, so tis said, so tis said,
>   Oh I killed a man tis said, that I hit him on the head,
> And I left him there for dead. Damn his hide!
>
> To the gallows I must go, I must go, I must go,
>   To the gallows I must go with my friends all down below
> Saying Sam, I told you so. Damn their hides!
>
> Oh, the preacher he did come, he did come, he did come,
>   Oh, the preacher he did come and he looked so very glum
> As he talked of Kingdom Come. Damn his hide!"

Dinny at last began to stir in the coffin. They began to wail loudly and keen and mourn. "Ah, poor Dinny. He was a good man, a brave man, he was. Let's drink to Dinny. Too bad he died! Let's sing another song for Dinny, poor soul."

Suddenly the little Irishman poked his head up out of the coffin, took a shocked look around and then went back into the box again. His four comrades laughed so hard they could hardly sing the last verse of Sammy Hall:

> "There was Nellie in the crowd, in the crowd, in the crowd
>   There was Nellie in the crowd and she looked so very proud,
> That I told her right out loud: Damn yer hide!"

Suddenly Dinny, by that time cold sober, jumped out of the coffin, punched Untu in the nose and Paddy in the eye and, grabbing an axe furiously drove them from the room. Then he smashed the coffin and the card table and two chairs before he sat down to nurse his wrongs, as any good Irishman would and should.

That was the end of the *Last Man Under the Table Club* but not the last of the tale. As you can imagine, the news of what happened spread joyously the length of the town before noon next day and most of the townspeople enjoyed it hugely. Nothing so exciting and hilarious had happened in Tioga for years. One person who did not find it at all amusing was Father Hassel, our Catholic priest. Still shaking from the experience of the night before, Dinny had come to him early next morning to confess his sins, and afterward he told the priest what had happened, that he really thought he was dead until he heard them laughing. "Ah, my son," said Father Hassel. "Once again I find that Our Dear Lord works his wonders in mysterious ways. You haven't been to confession for eleven years and I'd about given up all hope for you. I trust you will be at church come next Sunday, my son." Dinny promised that he would.

Then Father Hassel sent word to Paddy Feeny that he wanted to see him. When the blacksmith came the priest gave him billy blue hell. "Sacrilege! Sacrilege!" he roared and he told Paddy that his only chance of escaping eternal purgatory was to keep the churchyard and graveyard mowed and tidied up for two years. They needed it.

As for Dinny Callahan, no one had ever had such a mad on for so long a time as he brooded over what they'd done to him. The Irish have always cherished revenge. No one plays a dirty trick on an Irishman without paying for it. Unfortunately, all of the other members of the club were a lot bigger than Dinny and better fighters, too, as he found out at the post office when Untu innocently said, "Hi, Dinny, how are you?" hoping to make amends and perhaps get the club started again. Dinny interpreted the greeting as asking if he were still dead and laid into the big Finn, fists flying. Untu grabbed Dinny by the neck and threw him out of the post office door, then slugged him hard when he tried to fight some more. No, thought the Irishman. Some other way had to be found to get even.

Finally, he set out some traps in the swamp back of the slaughter house and caught four skunks, one for each of his tormenters. After the carcasses got ripe enough, and after slitting their stink glands to be sure they stunk enough, Dinny spent half a dark night dropping them through the holes of outhouses.

It wasn't enough, but it was something. Erin go braugh!

THE OLD TAILOR

Who's he? Old Fabian, our tailor.
He makes the whole town proud of him,
Of how he walks and carries eighty years.
You'd think his tailor's yard was in his coat,
The way he holds himself. Some say
He held a general's rank in Finland,
And had to flee when Russia took her freedom.
Whatever was his past, for twenty years,
He's worn that old brown derby helmet-like,
And marched, stiff-stepping down the hill to church.
You see that path he's shoveled from his house?
It's like him. Why, on his knees,
Beside his tailor's iron and dog-eared Bible,
I've seen him, heard him speak to God;
Andthoughthe tongue was strange, the tone
Was that of a proud soldier making his report
To the superior officer. He makes us proud.
Too proud perhaps, for but a week ago
To our back door he came, another man,
Old, broken, bent. I'd never thought to see him so.
Our cook translated: 'He has no wood.
He says he's had no fire for forty hours
And it's been twelve below. He's had not work.
The people tell him that he does things wrong.
He blames it on his eyes." She paused as he began,
Faltering, to speak again. The gutturals
Grew weak and trembling. Suddenly he wept.
It's hard to sit and watch a brave man cry.
'He says he's never had to ask for anything
From anyone before, but now he's old and sees not good.
And can you give him something he can do
In trade for wood and food? He hasn't
Eaten much, he says, for many weeks.'
When cook informed him what we told her to,
The old man said, 'I t'ank you.' and his
Hand crept to his head in effort to salute
In his old manner . . . but it failed.
He'd lost too much to manage it, you see,
Too much of his true self. And that's
The only tragedy of age. He'd conquered it
And kept himself intact until that day.
Now though he still goes marching down the street
As if in step to drums we cannot hear.
I fear the memory of that last defeat
Walks with him.

THE WHITE WOLF

eventy-five years ago there were many wolves in the U.P. though now they are almost extinct. All of us who lived in Tioga had heard them at night, usually in the deep of winter, when a wolf chased a deer out of the Buckeye and down through the big maple grove that covered the north side of our long hill. Their yapping and howling made the night ring with a wild eerie sound and we could almost follow the course of the pack as it pursued its quarry. Children shivered in their beds until the howling grew faint and finally was lost over the hills.

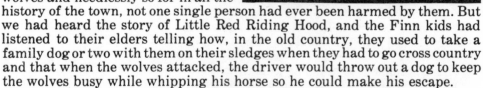

As children, all of us were fearful of wolves and needlessly so for in all the history of the town, not one single person had ever been harmed by them. But we had heard the story of Little Red Riding Hood, and the Finn kids had listened to their elders telling how, in the old country, they used to take a family dog or two with them on their sledges when they had to go cross country and that when the wolves attacked, the driver would throw out a dog to keep the wolves busy while whipping his horse so he could make his escape.

It was all nonsense of course. Timber wolves are either afraid of man, or more plausibly, they can't stand his adominable scent so they avoid contact with people if they possibly can. Rarely did we ever see one in the forest when hunting or fishing though we often saw wolf tracks in the snow or found the remains of a deer they had killed. Occasionally one of our deer hunters shot a wolf, or a trapper caught one or poisoned one, but not very often.

The possessor of a wolf skin coat was greatly envied. Indeed, if I remember right, there were only two such coats in Tioga. One was owned by Vic Toulon who had inherited it from his grandfather, a full blooded Menominee Indian. That coat was no beauty after all those years. It was mangy and moth ridden and held together in front by shingle nails and a loop of haywire but Vic was sure proud of it. The other coat, in contrast, was a beautiful garment, admired by all of us. It belonged to the best fur trapper in town, Eric Sippola, and the lustrous skins it was made of were from wolves that Eric had trapped or shot himself.

Our people couldn't understand how Eric managed to catch so many wolves until our blacksmith once gave away the secret, saying that he saved all the parings from the horses' hooves for him. Eric had told him that this particular bait overcame the wolves' intense cautiousness. Once the secret came out, other men too began to trap a few of them but it was still difficult work. You had to do it just right.

First, you had to boil your traps in a soup made of wild cherry bark and handle them with new or newly washed canvas gloves when you made your set at the base of a tree whose roots were spread far enough to leave a narrow hole between them. Then you put the hoof parings deep in the hole and one or two traps were placed and hidden in front of it. Eric always set his trap so that its pan was flush with the surface of a little indentation where a wolf would most likely put its right front foot if he tried to get at the bait. Then the trap was covered with sifted moss and leaves so it looked right natural. You had to know your stuff to catch a wolf.

Unlike the other Finns who lived on top of the hill, Eric's cabin was down in the valley, near the slaughter house. He was a nice man, about 35 years of age, and a bachelor. When some of us boys would go down to see him or the skins he had tacked onto his shed, he would give us a piece of hard cinnamon toast and tell us trapping stories. Since all of us did a little amateur trapping for biting money, we appreciated the lore he shared. He told us how to catch a weasel with a rat trap nailed to the bottom of a sapling; how to bury all but the tail of a sucker at the edge of a lake and then put your trap where a mink would have to step when it tried to dig it out; how to skin a skunk without getting stunk up too badly; how to stretch a muskrat hide over a round-ended board. Yes, we learned a lot from Eric and we missed him a lot after he shot the white wolf and then himself.

Stories about that white wolf had been around for two or three years. It roamed the area east of the old Hayshed Dam where the upper Tioga River tumbles through a gap in the granite hills. Rough country, completely wild and uncut, with rocky knobs, tangled alder swamps and a few lakes or streams. Except for some landlookers employed by the lumber companies, few people ever entered that wilderness. One of those who knew it well was Eric, who for some years had put a trap line through it all the way to Hell's Canyon in the Huron Mountains. He'd built a little overnight shack at the canyon so he could make his rounds every two days to check his traps.

At the post office one evening, Pitu Marsellies claimed that he had seen a white wolf, an arctic wolf, up by the Hayshed Dam and some of the other men were scoffing at the tale when Eric broke in. "That's right, Pitu," he said. "I seen that white wolf too, yes, three times I seen him, once close enough to see that he had pink eyes. An albino just like that white deer Laf Rafferty shot and brought to town four years ago. I tried last year to trap him but he's sure cagey. I'll get him this fall when the fur is prime. Bet that hide would go for a hundred dollars!"

And that fall, Eric tried hard, almost neglecting his traplines. Once getting a glimpse of white, he followed the wolf track in the early snow for two days, studying the wolf's habits. Probably rejected from the pack because of its color, the white wolf was a loner and a roamer. The track led all the way from Summit Lake to the headwaters of the Dead River and back again. Following it, Eric found where the wolf slept at night on top of a hemlock hill, where it caught and ate a rabbit, where it had crept up on a partridge and grabbed it just as it took off, where it followed a porcupine but decided not to tackle that ball of quills. Because of a deformed toe, the track of the white wolf was unmistakable.

One night, sleeping beside the trail, Eric had heard the white wolf's solitary howl, a deep throated tone that rose quivering in pitch a full octave, and was sustained there a full five seconds before coming down. Eric had often heard the wild music of a wolf pack in full cry, barking, yapping and yowling, but he had never known a howl like that of the white wolf, lone and lorn, there in the wilderness. The trapper put another log on the fire and felt for the gun under the blanket. But the howls gradually grew weaker and the time between them lengthened. "He's headed north now," said Eric to himself. "Maybe I can cut across and get on his trail . . . No, don't want to lose it."

Eric did his utmost that fall to trap the white wolf but failed, and when the deep drifts of winter came he had to give up. About the middle of March, however, he took up the quest again for wolves are hungrier early in the spring than at any other time and are more easily caught. At the same time he would go after beaver. Because of the daily thawing in late March, snowshoeing is so difficult that only at night, when the snow freezes hard again or early in the morning, can one walk without the terribly hard labor of lifting wet snow with every step. It is probable that Eric was snowshoeing after dark when he fell off a granite cliff onto some jagged rocks and broke his left leg in two pieces, one that pierced the skin.

We can't be sure what actually happened, but a timber cruiser for Silverthorne Lumber Company, who stumbled upon his body by sheer chance while looking for a lost forty of virgin pine, had this to say: "I was going south along the ridge when I come across snowshoe tracks, maybe two, three days old and heading right for the cliff. Curious, I followed them and seen where the poor bugger went right over it. I go round and back to the bottom of the hill and, Jeez, what a mess of old blood and thrashing around marks in the snow. Must have hurt him bad! And there was a wolf track I crossed before getting there, a big one. Well, I follow up the track where the man had crawled, leaving a trail of blood. How far? Mebbe four hundred yards and it must have took him two days of hell and you know, that wolf track was in his trail off and on. Probably knew the man was crippled bad. Finally, I seen Eric there in the snow with his head half blasted off. A mess. But before he shot himself, he got the wolf. Just one shot and right through the backbone, not fifty feet away. A white wolf. An albino."

APIL FOOL ON YOU, EMIL

In our little forest village of Tioga, April Fools Day was taken seriously, almost religiously. All day long you had to catch someone else and avoid being caught. Even the little kids would go to the window and cry out, "Hey ma, there's a robin. Come see!" though there were still patches of snow on the ground and the maple trees were just beginning to fill the sap buckets on their waists. Hell, the crows had just started to come back.

No one loved the day more than Emil Olsen, our town's practical joker. All year long he was always pulling some trick on someone. Why once he even greased the grave digger's shovel and laughed uproariously when the clods stuck to it instead of covering the casket. But April Fool was his day of days and his favorite victim was Eino Tuomi, his best friend and neighbor. Every year when the evening mail was being "disturbed" (distributed) in our little post office, Emil would be there in the anteroom telling all the tricks he'd played on Eino that day. "Oh, for stupid! Oh, for dumb! Eino, he fall for anything I do!" And then he'd tell how he put a horsehair in his pipe or salt in his sugar bowl, or glued the pages of the Sears Roebuck catalog together in his outhouse and nailed his barn boots to the floor. And more. Oddly enough, Eino never resented the tricks. He just said patiently, "You crazy, Emil. You nuts!"

But I'd better tell you something about these two characters so you can understand and appreciate how Emil finally got his comeuppance. Both had been hard ore drillers and had worked together for many years in the Oliver Iron Mining Company's deep Tioga mine until it suddenly shut down. Evidently the management had robbed the supporting pillars of ore that held up the overburden a bit too much. Anyway one afternoon when I was playing in the sideyard, a monstrous roar occurred, our new cement sidewalk cracked, and the house shook. A great cloud of dust obscured the sun. "Cave in! Cave in!"

All the people along our street streamed out of their houses and started running toward safety for they knew that the whole west end of town had been undermined. However, as things turned out, only an area about the size of a city block had collapsed but what a huge gaping hole remained. For years, we kids used to go gingerly to the edge of that hundred foot deep pit and wonder where the two men lay who had been buried in it.

Anyway, the mine shut down never to reopen and Eino and Emil were too old to hunt for work elsewhere so they stayed, eking out a precarious existence on tiny pensions and their own hard work. Perhaps an account of how they managed it will show you how our people survived hard times.

After the mine closed, Eino and Emil moved into two log cabins that had been abandoned. They were well built, snug structures of square hewn logs, warm in winter and cool in summer and they sat side by side across the street from the cave-in pit. Eino always had two old chairs in his front yard and it was there that the two old men would sit on a summer's day smoking their corncob pipes and arguing. Always arguing. Why they'd even argue about which bird would fly off the telephone line first.

Eino, the Finn, was a small but wiry man with a soft voice but Emil, the Swede, was a huge fellow with a voice like a bull. You could hear him bellowing all the way from Flinn's store. At first, I thought they were mad at each other, but instead, they were great friends, almost inseparable. They had evolved a symbiotic way of living that really worked. Eino had a barn behind his house and kept a cow; Emil had a chickenhouse and a big garden full of potatoes, rutabagas and cabbage which both helped till. They shared everything and we never saw one without the other. Why, when Eino's cow had to be serviced by Mr. Sulu's bull, they both held the rope that led it, almost hand in hand. Didn't bother them a bit when the usual bystander made the usual bawdy remarks about their mission. (I always hated that job when I had to take Rosie, our Jersey cow, to the Sulu's bull. It was interesting once I got there, but oh, how everybody kidded me along the route. "Wassa matter, Cully? Why you no do it yourself?" (Stuff like that.)

So they had milk and butter and eggs and occasionally they stewed a tough old rooster all day and night on the kitchen stove. Or if the gods were good, they had real meat from a young steer they'd raised instead of the usual illicit venison. Once Eino traded a calf for two of Delong's young pigs but the bear got them before they could be butchered. Besides berries, the only fresh fruit they ate were apples they had picked from a tree at one of the abandoned houses. And they had fish, of course, fresh trout or pike in the summer and smoked or marinated for the long white of winter. They didn't fish much with hook or line for the trout though. Instead, as they showed me once, they'd take a stick of dynamite, a blasting cap, and length of white fuse, put it on a raft in a promising beaver dam, light the fuse and run like hell. Then they'd scoop up all the trout, suckers and chubs, put them in gunny sacks and dump them uncleaned, guts and all, into the marinating barrels in their cellars. Almost every family in town had dynamite after the mine closed. Very useful in making a new outhouse hole or getting rid of a big stump. We kids used to have fun throwing chunks of ore at a blasting cap trying to get it to go off until once one did and Nicky Johnson lost an arm.

For the necessaries, the two old men had to have some biting money and that came from odd jobs or the thirty dollars pension checks that came to them each month. I was up at M.C. Flinn's store once when they came there to have the checks cashed. Emil, who could neither read nor write, always got red faced when he had to put his mark (X) on the check and when Mr. Flinn wrote "Emil Olsen, his mark. M.C. Flinn, storekeeper" under it. They always bought the same stuff: a pail of Peerless smoking tobacco, two dozen circular discs of black rye hardtack, a bag of korpua (a dried toast flavored with cinnamon), coffee, sugar and salt, a chunk of salt pork, and a half slab of bacon. Once a year they bought a sack of flour and some baking soda for their pancakes. Like all of us, they made their own maple syrup, so all in all they ate well and lived well. Nobody thought of them as being poor, nor did they.

On the afternoon of the last day of March one year, I had been selling copies of *Grit* up and down the street to my regular customers and somehow had an extra copy left, so I thought I'd give it to Eino who could read fine. I'd done that before and was always rewarded by having them tell me stories of mining in the old days or hearing them argue over something in the magazine. I could hear them hard at it by the time I got to Flinn's store. With a brace and bit, Eino was drilling a hole in the telephone post beside his house and Emil was giving him hell.

"Oh, for dumb!" he was yelling. "You no get any sap from telephone pole. It dead wood. It got no roots. Eino, you crazy dumb!" The little Finn was not bothered at all. "Oh, yah, I get sap. Best sweet sap. More sweet than maple tree give."

"No!" roared Emil. "Look, dummy. Hole is dry. Pole is spruce, dead spruce. It no give sap, stupid! Oh, for dumb!" Eino, unperturbed, took a length of elderberry stalk out of his pocket, slit it in half, scraped out the pith to make a little trough, hammered the spike into the hole and hung a pail from it. "Sure, Emil," he said. "No sap now. It come at night. You see in morning I get pail full." They were still arguing when I left, but I heard Eino say, "I make pancakes tomorrow for new syrup. You come eat my house, Emil. Bring eggs. I got sour milk."

According to the way Eino told the tale at the post office that next evening, on his way to breakfast, Emil had stopped at the telephone pole, put a finger first in the sap pail and then in his mouth. His face red with fury, he charged to the chair where Eino was sitting. "You sunabits, Eino, you peed in sap can. I going bust you in nose!"

Eino didn't get up. "Apil Fool, Emil! Apil Fool. Old Eino, he not so dumb!"

SUMMER ROMANCE

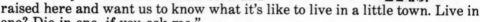

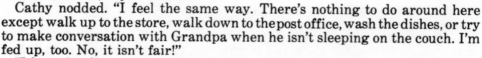

My two girls, Cathy, 16 and Susan, 14, were bellyaching as they sat miserably on the front steps of their grandfather's house.

"Ugh! What a dump to be stuck in," said Sue. She was almost crying. "We've been here a whole week with five more weeks to go," she wailed. "Don't know about you, Cathy, but I've had it up to here. I want to go home. It's not fair for Dad to drag us up to this dead hole in the woods just because he was born and raised here and want us to know what it's like to live in a little town. Live in one? Die in one, if you ask me."

Cathy nodded. "I feel the same way. There's nothing to do around here except walk up to the store, walk down to the post office, wash the dishes, or try to make conversation with Grandpa when he isn't sleeping on the couch. I'm fed up, too. No, it isn't fair!"

"It's easier for you than for me, Cathy. You at least can write Tim every day . . ."

"And never get any answer." Cathy was angry. "We've been here six days now and no mail at all. Maybe he's fooling around with that dumb red head while I'm gone. The least he could do is send me a note. Oh, I hate men."

"Well, I don't, said Sue. "That's part of what's wrong. There just don't seem to be any boys up here. Not our age anyway. There must be some of them hiding in the bushes somewhere, probably covered with moss. Even down at the beach where we go swimming you only see little kids. Haven't they got any older brothers or do the natives up here leave as soon as they can shave? Wouldn't blame them, at that. I want to go home.

Cathy had been thinking. "Hey Sue, how about this? Let's have a heart to heart talk with Dad and tell it to him straight - that we just can't stand being up here any longer, that we're sick of it, and want him to take us home. We're old enough now so that if he wants to come back with Mom to do some more fishing, we can take care of ourselves."

Sue was not impressed. "Not a chance," she said. "He still thinks of us as little kids. But if all of us, and I mean John too, say we want to go back and keep talking about it, maybe we won't have to stay here so long. Hey, here comes John now." She pointed up the street to their younger brother.

"Hey, John, come here." The boy came over and sat on the steps with his sisters as they explained.

"Nope, not me." he replied. "I don't want to go home. I'm having fun up here. Jeez, we've sure been having fun playing Duck on the Rock. You put one rock on another big one and choose up sides and then one guy knocks it off . . ."

"Knock it off, yourself," Sue said in exasperation. "Maybe you're having fun but we sure aren't." She began to cry a little. Sue could always turn on the tears when needed, but John wasn't impressed.

"Nope. No you don't. Bawl yer head off, but I'm staying here. You know what they've got down in the grove? They got a big cable they found up at the old mine and it's strung between two big trees and you climb up one of them and sit down on a seat that's under a pulley and wow, what a ride! Scary! Really neat! I'll show you where it is sometimes - if I have time. Gotta get my ball now. Nope. I'm staying up here as long as I can." He left them, whistling.

"Well," said Cathy, "Let's face it, Sue. We're stuck here for the rest of the summer. Wait . . . I've got an idea. John! John!" she called.

Her brother came to the door. "Whatcha want?"

"Who are you going to play baseball with - and where do you play?" Cathy asked her brother.

"Oh, there's a bunch of us kids. There's a men's team here that plays against other towns each Sunday and they practice against us kids on Saturday, tomorrow. We thought we'd get ready for them, do some batting, and practice on fly balls and grounders. They got a diamond up there by the old mine. "Bye."

"Wait a minute, Bullet Head. How do you get there? Any big kids on your team?"

"Yeh, my friend Davy has a big brother, Jimmy, who plays with us, and there are a couple of other high school guys. I already told you — it's up by the mine. You know, by the big tall building with the wheels on top. Up there. I gotta hurry."

"Wait, we'll go with you," said Sue.

"Oh no you won't. I'm going by myself. Don't want any big sisters tagging along. Nuts to you." And John ran up the street.

The two girls looked at each other. "OK," said Sue. "Let's go looking." They giggled all the way up to the mine. The diamond was just a cow pasture with gunny sacks for bases. No bleachers. So they sat demurely on a rock and watched, occasionally applauding a good hit or catch and whispering to each other that there really were two or three possibilities, "that short blonde one over there and the one with light brown hair who looks like he's part Indian."

That evening after supper the girls cornered John. "Who was that short blonde guy, the one who fell down when he stumbled on the bag?"

"That was Tommy. He's a character. Always saying something to break us up."

"Who's that neat one that hit the ball into the creek?"

"That's Jimmy, Davy's brother. He plays basketball too. One of the guys has a rope hanging from a tree branch in his yard - must be twenty feet long - and Jimmy can climb that thing using only his hands."

"Did any of the guys ask you what our names were?"

"Naw."

The next afternoon both girls skipped swimming to watch the practice game between the boys and the town men's team. Again they were the only spectators and again were ignored despite their applause for the one weak hit made by the younger players. A rout. Moreover, these efforts seemed to have been completely in vain. Nothing happened the rest of the week. Jimmy and Tommy never appeared. Nor any other boys. Several times each day Cathy and Sue spent hours carefully dressing and grooming themselves before walking up and down the hill street. Each afternoon they swam in the lake, lay as attractively as possible on the beach, or paraded back and forth across it. No boy even remotely their age showed up. Just a lot of little kids, six to ten, all of whom John seemed to know well. Sometimes on their jaunts Cathy and Sue would occasionally encounter a pair of high school girls who stared at them impassively when they tentatively offered a friendly smile, then giggled after they had gone by. Utter abominable misery, day after day. The girls constantly begged us to take them home.

As usual it was Cathy who first faced up to the situation. "I guess Jimmy and Tommy or any of the other boys our age aren't going to come to us. We're just going to have to go where they are." she said to Sue.

"If you ask me, they're hiding under some rock somewhere, the cockroaches," said Sue. "We'd have to overturn every boulder and beat every bush around this lousy town to find even one and then he'd probably run away. Nuts to 'em. Let's just take off and hitchhike home, Cathy. I just can't stand it another minute."

"Listen, Sue. You know we're stuck here and besides, I've got another idea. Maybe what we've got to do is work through their little brothers and sisters. Make friends with them and maybe they'll show us those rocks where the big guys hide." Cathy grinned.

That's exactly what my daughters did. They promised John that they'd be good to him for once, that they'd make chocolate fudge or popcorn or cookies for his friends if he could get them to come down to Grandpa's porch after supper. The bait worked. By the end of the week a motley group of little kids, boys and girls alike, were coming for their snacks and having fun chasing one another around the yard, chattering and laughing on the front steps. Cathy and Sue presided with skill over these nightly gatherings, learned all the kids' names, got them to talking about themselves (and their older brothers) and answering a thousand questions about how it was to live and go to school in a real city.

Every evening the two girls were queens holding court. To the village children they were glamorous creatures from another world, yet who were really interested in them and how they lived. The word got around - Cathy and Sue weren't a bit "stuck up." They were friendly and they were fun. Indeed, so many kids began to show up that Grandpa began to grumble at the noise and chased them all away when the clock struck nine.

It didn't take much of this before my daughters were never able to be alone even when they wanted to be. We began to call them the Pied Piperettes for rarely could they get more than a block from the house on their walks before an entourage would begin to assemble. When they asked about Sliding Rock or Mount Baldy or the old iron furnace by the waterfall, there was always a group of youngsters to lead them there. Sue and Cathy even visited some of the boys' hideaway shacks in the grove to dutifully admire the piles of stones stored up as ammunition for fights that were sure to come. Together with the kids they scratched their names on Writing Rock up on Mount Baldy and marvelled at the ski jump the older boys had constructed.

When Sue and Cathy mentioned that they wished they could get to see the bears at the dump they were told marvelous stories about how the bears came to town in the fall to raid the apple trees, and what happened next. Sue and Cathy even learned how to swing from birch saplings on the edge of the hill, to eat raspberry tucks and nibble wintergreen leaves. Then one day, Davy, John's special friend, asked them to come up to his house to see his pet skunk. When they did, there were Jimmy and Tommy sharpening a scythe on the grindstone. My daughter Sue managed to ask Davy a lot of questions. How had and who had caught the skunk? (Jimmy had when it got tangled in the chickenwire.) Who had de-scented it? (Old Pullapin with a jackknife.) Before they knew it all of them were talking as though they had always known each other, Jimmy and Tommy included.

When Sue and Cathy got back that afternoon they were higher than steeples, laughing and jabbering secretly with each other, completely triumphant and very happy. That evening I noticed that there were older boys on the edge of the porch when dusk came to our village.

The remaining weeks of that summer went by very swiftly for all of us. Even today, many years later, the two girls remember that period as one of the best times of their lives. Tommy and Sue, Cathy and Jimmy were together every hour they could manage. I don't know what they did or didn't. All I know is that every morning the girls shampooed and set their hair in rollers, washed and ironed their dresses for the evening, laughed and giggled constantly or whispered to each other whenever I came by. They refused to go with us to our old hunting cabin; they didn't want to go swimming at the beach.

About dusk Sue and Cathy disappeared completely and when they returned about midnight they were always radiant. Their mother told me not to pry - as though I would have. I knew they thought that they were in love. Thank heaven it was about time to go home. I think my wife worried a bit too obviously once because Sue felt she had to reassure her. "Mom, Jimmy and Tommy are so darned shy, it's painful. All we do is talk and talk and talk. They keep asking us all about what it's like back home or telling us how someday they're going to escape and do great things. Or we go exploring. Things like that. Don't you and Dad worry. I tell you these boys are unbelievably shy. Terrible!" Sue had collected the scalps of half the boys in her high school but she told us she had never met any like these from the backwoods.

Finally it came time to depart. The morning before we left, and quite accidentally, I overheard the two of them talking in the bathroom. "I cried myself to sleep last night," said Sue. "I can't bear to go now. I love Tommy, I really do. And you know he hasn't even kissed me yet, Cathy. I could have killed him last night, he's so awkward and shy. Have I got bad breath or something? But I'll get him tonight even if I have to wrap my arms around him and throw him to the ground. Darn him anyway!"

"I know. I know," Cathy responded. "Jimmy's the same way. They've been in the woods too much or something. But we've got one more evening together. Only one. Only one!" I could hear both girls weeping.

Cathy and Sue were on edge all day. I did not dare do my usual teasing about their hair dressing and primping and when I insisted that they pack their bags so we could get an early start next morning they turned on me in a fury. Hour after hour they got touchier, nastier, and all through the supper meal they were withdrawn and surly. It was therefore with some appreciative amusement that I saw and heard them suddenly change into gay bubbling spirits once Jimmy and Tommy came through the gate to get them.

For the first time the two couples walked away hand in hand. A last evening together with moonlight flickering down through the maples over the sidewalk. I tried to remember what it was like but couldn't. So wishing them well in their kissing I finished loading the car. Couldn't get to sleep though, so I was down in the kitchen having a midnight bowl of cornflakes when they burst into the house, right on the stroke of twelve according to our previous agreement, Sue from the back door and Cathy from the woodshed. Both were rubbing their mouths and when they saw each other doing it, they doubled up in a fit of uncontrollable laughter.

It was years later before I found the reason why. Both of the girls had indeed gotten their farewell kisses but both of the boys had been chewing snuff. I used to chew it too when I was their age. Made me feel tough and manly. Gave me courage.

BEARS, BEARS, BEARS

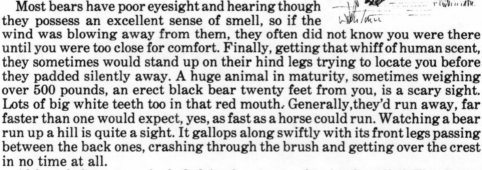

No account of life in the old U.P. would be complete without some mention of bears. I daresay there wasn't a single one of the inhabitants of Tioga who had not seen or encountered them repeatedly. Every fall they raided our gardens and apple trees. Every year someone had a pig taken by bears. That was one reason that old Mrs. Murphy always kept her Paddy pig in her bedroom every night. When we picked blueberries or sugar plums, bears were picking them too so we always kept a wary eye out for some big black shape in the bushes. Not that they were usually dangerous, but it wasn't wise to surprise them.

Most bears have poor eyesight and hearing though they possess an excellent sense of smell, so if the wind was blowing away from them, they often did not know you were there until you were too close for comfort. Finally, getting that whiff of human scent, they sometimes would stand up on their hind legs trying to locate you before they padded silently away. A huge animal in maturity, sometimes weighing over 500 pounds, an erect black bear twenty feet from you, is a scary sight. Lots of big white teeth too in that red mouth. Generally, they'd run away, far faster than one would expect, yes, as fast as a horse could run. Watching a bear run up a hill is quite a sight. It gallops along swiftly with its front legs passing between the back ones, crashing through the brush and getting over the crest in no time at all.

Although bears are included in the group of animals called The Seven Sleepers, they do not truly hibernate, as Mulu Ankinen found out one afternoon early in March. He'd been snowshoeing across country to check out a beaver pond where he could set some traps and under a big windfall lodged against a granite outcropping he saw the black back of a sleeping bear. Thinking it was still hibernating, he poked it with a stick and out it came with a tremendous growl. Mulu turned and ran, of course, but it's hard running on snowshoes. He fell and lay there playing dead while the she bear sniffed him all over. Finally, she turned and went back to the den and Mulu, shaken by the experience, returned to town. The next day, armed with his deer rifle, he retraced his steps and shot her where she lay. A big sow bear with two little cubs barely eight inches long.

Bears have their young in February and March and the cubs nurse the mother until spring, even as she sleeps. They remain with her for about a year and a half, but then are driven off to fend for themselves. I've said that bears were not usually dangerous but this is not true of a mother bear with cubs. Most of the bear maulings of humans is done by sow bears with young. I almost got in trouble myself one time when I tried to take a picture of a cub that had climbed up an old pine stub. I never saw the mother but I heard her growl before I ran.

Arvo and Arne Mattila almost got it too when they found three young cubs playing and boxing each other on the shore of Lake Tioga. After some trouble and a lot of squealing, they captured the cubs, put them in a burlap sack, and started to take them to town thinking they might be able to sell them to the zoo on Presque Isle in Marquette. But the mother bear, hearing the squalling, showed up and made for the two Finns. Just in the nick of time, they managed to jump into their boat and row toward Flat Island and what they thought was safety. But bears are good swimmers and the she bear dived into the water after them and the gunnysack that held her yelping young.

What to do? Arvo and Arne didn't want to be caught on that little island with a mad mother bear, so, counting on the bear's poor eyesight and hearing, they rowed like the devil in a big circle downwind and back to the mainland. They said the mother was still swimming toward the island when they got ashore. I don't know what happened to the cubs. Arvo and Arne brought them over to our house to show my dad and ask his advice. (He told them to take them back to their mother, but I doubt if they did.) Anyway, the cubs sure were fun to watch once they'd gotten over their fright. About three feet long and weighing maybe forty pounds apiece, they frolicked and tumbled all over our yard and ate the bread and honey we put out for them. Almost human.

Marcel Pitou said that once he had been chased up a birch tree by a sow bear and that when it climbed up after him, he was able to kick it hard in the nose with his boot. He'd heard that a bear's nose is its Achilles heel, the most sensitive part of its body. Anyway, the bear went down the tree, hung around at its base for a while growling, but finally went away.

Stories like these did not bother most of us who spent a lot of time in the woods. We respected bears but did not fear them. Indeed, they feared us and would always avoid us when they could. Perhaps they disliked man scent almost as much as we were repelled by theirs. When they had crossed one of our paths along the river, they left a rank odor that would linger for hours where they had passed. I remember vividly how once when Grampa Gage and I were driving Billy and the buckboard up an old logging road to go trout fishing, the horse had stopped suddenly with ears back and white eyes rolling, backing and filling and refusing to go onward until Grampa got off the rig and led it. Bear smell! Moreover, four hours later on our return trip, Billy did the same thing at the same spot.

A solitary animal, often nocturnal, you rarely saw more than one bear at a time but old man Takkinen claimed he once saw seven of them in a group one October, just before they paired off and mated. He said they were sniffing and some of the males were cuffing each other. After mating occurs, the males always go their own way. Never did anyone ever find two big bears in the same den.

Occasionally, however, especially when there had been a poor crop of berries, we saw several bears at the town garbage dump at the same time but even then the biggest one would chase the others away until it had had its fill. They didn't fraternize at all. They walked by their wild lone.

Many of the townspeople, especially the women and kids, however, were very afraid of the critters. Once when we had a half grown bear up a clump of maple trees in our front yard near our front porch, my Grama Gage almost went crazy with the fright of it. She locked her bedroom door, pulled down the curtains, and then spent most of a long afternoon peering along the edges to make sure the bear was still in the tree. "Why don't you shoot it, John? Why don't you shoot it before it jumps to the porch and breaks through my window?" she asked my father. Instead, Dad got a plate of sardines and put some in the crotch of a lower branch which the cub came down to eat before it took off down the street with a posse of barking dogs and yelling kids in pursuit.

Dad liked bears but that didn't prevent him from shooting a big one once when deer hunting. Its glossy black hide and head he had made into a rug. We never used it on the floor but had it hung over the unused door into the back hall stairway. As children we used to poke its glass eyes and shiveringly put our fingers into its snarling mouth when we felt brave enough.

Most of the bears that our townspeople killed were raiding our apple trees or /private garbage dumps. The township picked up all the garbage once a year in the spring but by fall each house had it own pile of cans and stuff by the barn or outhouse so the bears had good pickings. Usually they came by night and we'd go out the next morning to see the mess they'd left, and their footprints. The latter looked almost like those of a huge man. You could see the five toes and the heel but it was wide, not as narrow as a man's track. Bears walk like a man does but on all fours, putting the heel down first before the toes. We could tell how big a bear was by his prints. One huge bear left footprints as big as a dinner plate in our garden dirt one fall and Dad estimated its weight as being over 600 pounds.

The biggest bear I ever saw came out of the brush and entered the big pool under the old Rolling Null logging dam on the west branch of the Tioga. I was no more than a hundred feet downstream flyfishing for trout when it appeared, so I froze motionless as it proceeded to catch some big redhorse suckers. The bear would thrash around in the water, then suddenly poke its head under and come up with a big one in its jaws. Then he'd sit down in the water, hold it in both forepaws and eat it like a stalk of celery. Because I was downwind, that bear never knew I was there. It was an enormous animal and I could feel the hair on my neck tingle when once it turned and looked directly at me. Also, I was sure relieved when, after dining on three big suckers, it loped away. I swear that bear was eight feet long with muscles on its muscles.

Few people appreciate how powerful bears are. One of our French Canadians, Raoul Decroix, sure did. One fall, just before he was ready to butcher a two hundred pound hog, a bear broke down the pig pen and made off with it. Raoul got his rifle and trailed that bear two miles before he lost the track in a swamp. None of us could figure how that bear could do it. How did he hold that hog? Surely not in his mouth. On three legs, holding it with the fourth?

Another French Canadian, Pierre Toulouse, told of watching a bear run down a crippled deer and break its neck with one mighty swat of a forepaw. I know that bears can kill deer for I saw one eating on a deer carcass up by Brown's Dam. Of course, it's possible that the deer had died from disease or something else for bears like carrion of any kind. Maybe that's why they smell so bad.

Arvo Mattila had a camp up at the junction of Blaney Creek and the Tioga. It was well built of heavy logs and had a good roof of boards covered with sheets of galvanized iron. No one had been in it all summer. When Arvo went there to take supplies for deer season, he yelled, "Vandals! Der's been vandals here!" for half the roof was stripped off, the door was hanging ajar, and a mattress had been hauled out in front. Inside was an incredible mess. Cans and bottles and frying pans were all over the floor. Chairs were broken. The stove pipe was wrecked; the table was overturned. But vandals had not done it. There were bear tracks and claw prints everywhere.

I myself witnessed a big bear overturn a huge and solid pine stump, break it off from its tough roots and haul it ten feet away to get at the grubs or ants that infested it. Five men couldn't have done it even with crowbars. Bears seem to be especially fond of red ants. An old Indian who lived down by the tracks told me "It's dere pepper. Dey need it when dey been eating rotten meat." Bears also like honey and seem impervious to bee stings when robbing a nest. They eat the bees too.

More bears around our village were killed by the Finns than by those of other nationalities, perhaps because their folklore had many tales of evil spirits assuming the shape of the bear, or of men who had been turned into bears by some sorcerer. Bears are hard to hunt because they travel far in the forest and are always moving. Also, in the winter they leave no tracks in the snow because they're asleep. In the spring and summer their fur is often mangy and you have to wait till early fall when it is prime enough to make the bearskin caps and coats that the Finns wore so proudly.

Some of them ate the bear meat and I have too. It is very dark, almost black, and you have to be sure to get rid of the fat or you'll gag on it. Meat from an old bear is terribly tough and tastes like boot leather but that from a half grown cub is quite palatable, having a taste that is halfway between beef and pork. We usually parboiled it before roasting. Pan fried bear steaks usually went into the outhouse hole.

Under their black hides, bears have a heavy layer of fat and this was often rendered down by our people to make bear grease for our boots. It was an excellent waterproofing agent when rubbed hard into the leather but it smelled terrible. My friends, however, didn't seem to mind it at all. Nor did Alphonse Valois who used it to keep his unruly black hair smoothed down. When he asked Arminda Paquette for a date, she put it eloquently, "Non, non, Alphonse, you stink like a bear!" He did. When he left the anteroom of the post office, he left his odor behind.

I guess that's about enough about bears. Except for one tale that Slim Jim Vester, our town liar, used to tell. He said he'd taken his horse and buckboard up to the Granite Plains after blackberries. "I allus take my gun along," he said. "Those bear, you can't trust 'em come berry time. Well, I'd got my ten quart pail half full when up comes a big old he bear aslavering and grunting. Wanted my berries. So I ups and shot him right in the ear three, four times. Fur didn't look so bad so I took my pail and rifle back to the buckboard and went back to skin 'im out. Big hide; Mister. Tried lugging it by the tail but it keep ketching on every bush so I ups and puts it over my back and shoulders. Waal, I hadn't got more 'n fifty yards when a big old sow bear comes out of the bushes and blocks my way. I says Howdy and starts walking polite around the critter but she rars up and blocks my way again. You know what, Mister? I had to screw that old sow bear four times afore she let me pass."

That's enough about bears.

TWENTY-SEVENTH LETTER OF THE ALPHABET

om Helet and Mary Modine were born twenty minutes apart on the same day of the same year in houses that sat side by side on our village hill street. From that beginning, their lives were entwined for eighteen years. As babies, they played on the floors of both houses while their mothers shared gossip over the morning coffee cups.

Until they went to school, the boy and girl were inseparable companions and they remained that way through first grade. With entrance into second grade came the cruel jeers that enforced the first law of childhood: boys play with boys and girls with girls. Tom felt the social pressure first and was outraged when Mary came to his assistance and yanked at the hair of the other boy with whom he was fighting. He didn't appreciate her help. "Leave me alone!" he yelled at her. "I'm not going to play with you no more! I hate you!"

But she wouldn't let him alone. If he walked up the street, she tagged along. If he played in the yard, she appeared. The more he rejected her, the more she sought his attention, any attention, good or bad. It was always bad. In school they competed furiously, taking turns having the better report card. Always Mary chose Tommy as her partner whenever this was possible. She always managed to sit near him and made his life miserable. Finally, he hit her a good one. It was a mistake because, being bigger than he was, she beat him up.

What was worst of all, Mary teased him unmercifully about his ears which did stick out a bit. "Elephant ears! Elephant ears! Jug ears! Hi Jug!" The latter became his nickname and soon was adopted by everyone - even occasionally by his mother - and every time he heard it, Tommy hated Mary with a passion. He used to daydream about putting her in a wire cage with legs and hands tied and only her neck sticking out. And then he'd put in some rats and watch gleefully as they chewed her up.

Only once had he really gotten some revenge. In the fourth grade the school put on a program at the Town Hall on May Day. They'd set up a May Pole with paper streamers coming down from its top, each held by a boy or girl who skipped and sang as they circled and wound the streamers about the pole. Though the dance had been practiced thoroughly and well, Tommy disgraced himself by giving Mary a good kick in the butt as she passed him in the final round. She screamed and socked him and the whole program was a disaster. He got a good licking when he got home.

To get away from her, at least in school, Tommy went to the principal and asked to skip the fifth grade, saying it was too easy and that he was bored. Surprisingly, his request was granted and for a month Tommy had some peace. Then Mary was promoted too, finagled a desk just in front of his own, teasing him more than ever. Once, when he dipped her pigtails in his inkwell, she didn't tattle to the teacher but told her mother who told his mother and Tommy got another licking.

In the seventh grade, when all the other kids were covertly exchanging mushy notes, those that went between Tommy and Mary were only insulting. "Dear Tommy: If you were in a boat on Lake Tioga, you wouldn't need any oars. Just your ears and some wind. Love, Mary." To which he replied, "Mary, you are a dog. Not yours, Tommy." That sort of thing.

By the eighth grade, Tommy had discovered that girls had legs and that Mary had pretty ones. He hated himself when he found himself looking at them. Once at a party where they played spin-the-bottle, Mary had kissed him so enthusiastically, he kept thinking about it even when he was trout fishing. And, for the first time, Tommy didn't burn up the valentine she sent him but hid it in one of the books in his bedroom.

It was in his junior year in High School, though, that he surrendered. Mary had seen him practicing some waltz steps on the sidewalk one afternoon after school and offered to teach him to dance not only the waltz but the foxtrot and two-step as well. "We've got a victrola, Tommy," she said. "My mother's gone to Ishpeming on the train and there's no one home. I can teach you." Somehow he let himself be persuaded. The session went better than he'd expected but that night Tommy didn't sleep well. The insides of his arms kept remembering how Mary felt when they held her.

The lessons continued, almost every other day, until he felt confident enough to ask her if he could take her to the Junior Prom. She refused. "No, Tommy. All the girls have decided to go as a group but if you want to sign my program when we get there, I may save a dance or two for you." He was furious. "What the hell do I care? What the hell do I care!" he told himself over and over. "I'll dance with the other girls, and to hell with Mary!" But when the time came and he found that her program had only one empty space for his name, for the last dance of the evening, he took what he could get, and didn't dance with anyone else. Just hung around in the corner with the other stags, glowering at each of her partners until his turn came. It was a waltz that seemed to end almost before it began. The two of them could have danced on forever. Almost like floating, he thought, floating with the prettiest girl in town in his arms. Tommy walked Mary home with the moonlight flickering through the maples overhead but when they stood there in the doorway, uncertain and awkward, he could not get up nerve enough to kiss her goodnight. Instead he bolted and ran away, walking the streets for an hour shivering with delight. He felt immensely tall, as though his head were brushing stars.

The next evening Tommy asked Mary to come with him to see Orion's Belt in the sky. They took the back road over to Mt. Baldy where they sat for a long time on Lover's Rock holding hands. When finally Mary said it was time to go back, he told her the tale of the twenty-seventh letter of the alphabet. It was called the sodoredo, he said, and he scratched its name with a piece of quartz on some shale. It looked like a short bar ringed on each end with a circle. It was Chinese, he said, the only Chinese letter in the alphabet. And then Tommy told her a wild imaginative tale about the ancient Emperor Tang who was utterly bored and unhappy because he had seen everything and done everything. "Find me a new pleasure or off with your head!" was his command to Ko-fu, the chief counselor. "You have one month only. Begone!"

Fearing for his life, Ko-fu journeyed to the far reaches of the empire seeking the new pleasure but in vain. Finally, when the month was almost up, he went into a great forest to hide and was starving when he met a poorly dressed, but beautiful, young woman sitting on a log sucking a chicken bone. "Food! Food!" Ko-fu cried. "No," said the woman. "I am starving too. You can't have my chicken bone but you can suck on the other end of it if you wish." Ko-fu did so and finally their sucking lips met. An electric shock traveled up his spine. "Hai, Hai!" he shouted. "I have the Emperor's new pleasure!"

After he tried out the chicken bone on his five hundred concubines, the great Emperor Tang was so delighted he decreed that all the chickens in China were to be reserved for the Imperial Court, and all their bones for the royal lips alone. But the people soon discovered that they didn't need a chicken bone to perform what they called the sodoredo, that all that was required was a man and a maid with their lips touching.

It was then that Tommy kissed Mary for the first time. Over and over again they practiced making the twenty-seventh letter of the alphabet until the moon was overhead and they were exhausted. On their way home, Mary asked Tommy why he called it the sodoredo in his story. "Oh," he replied. "There's a forest bird that always sings 'sol-doh-re-doh'. Somehow every time I hear it, I think of you." Tommy whistled the notes. It became their secret call to each other.

Their senior year in High School sped by as swiftly as that last dance of the Junior Prom. Tom and Mary were together constantly. They wandered the old logging trails as well as our hill street hand in hand, caring not who saw them. They got up at dawn to cook a little breakfast together at one of their special places along a stream or lake. They studied together but did not sleep together. Tom brought Mary daisies with all petals removed except one. They collected minerals and wildflowers, birds and stars. Not once did they have a lover's quarrel. It was a year of unutterable delight. It ended too soon.

As that last idyllic summer after graduation came to a close, Tommy made preparations to go to the University of Michigan in Ann Arbor. He would have to get a part-time job for board and room but had enough money to pay the tuition. The last weeks were full of sweet agony for both of them as the separation came closer. They swore the ancient vows of eternal fidelity. They made plans. After he got his degree and a job, they would be married and have children and live happy-ever-after. Mary would wait for him. He would hitchhike home for Christmas. There were tears in their twenty-seventh letters of the alphabet. They were not to see each other again for more than half a century. . . .

As Tom Helet drove his big car northward toward the Mackinac Bridge, he was not thinking of Mary Modine. After all, fifty-one years had passed since he'd been in the U.P. That chapter in his life had long been closed. Shortly after he had left to go to the university, Mary and her family had moved to California. The letters between them, at first so full of yearning, had gradually petered out. She had married and so had he. No, the reason for his growing excitement was that he was going home, home to the old U.P. to start a new life. Retirement had been hard on Tom, not because of financial reasons - there was a big pension and royalties from the two inventions - but mainly because he felt lonely and useless. His wife had died three years before and two weeks of visiting his daughter and grandchildren up in Maine had been one week too long. Though his son was stationed in England, Tom had no urge to travel. That was why, when the letter from Reino Bissola arrived at his New York condominium offering to sell him the old family home in Tioga, Tom decided to buy it and spend the rest of his days in the land of his youth. The old house had been left to his sister who had sold it to Reino. It was in good condition, Reino wrote, but needed painting and a new roof. Good! Give him something to do. And he could hunt and fish again. Tom sent a check to hold it, made tentative arrangements to sell the condominium, packed his clothes and was on his way. On his way back to Tioga and the U.P.!

Suddenly at the end of a long stretch of road, he saw a shimmering silver structure that almost seemed to be floating in the sky, the Mackinac Bridge. Soon he was on it, the tires snarling on the gratings, with a glimpse of a huge ore-carrier floating down below. Exhilaration rippled up Tom's spine. There's the U.P.! Going home! Going home! Clear lakes and streams! Clean air - and the spruce and balsam and birch of his boyhood! Fifty-one years - but now he was back where he belonged. Tom even found it hard to stop for gas. Go where the wild goose goes! Go, go, go! All the doubts about the wisdom of his decision faded away. He took the old road on which he'd hitchhiked so long ago rather than the newer U.S. 2 even though the gas station attendant said the latter was much more beautiful since it ran closer to Lake Michigan. No, he was retracing his steps, erasing them. At Trout Lake he bought a pasty and a bottle of ketchup and sat on a little side road under a big hemlock tree as he ate it. Tom thought about Mary for the first time. She had baked him a pasty for the other trip fifty-one years before, and he had eaten that one under a hemlock tree too. Yawning, he dozed a bit there in the sun before going on. It was good, very, very good to be going home.

At McMillan he turned west on M-28. Again he thought of Mary when he saw signs telling of the Tahquamenon Falls, the place they had once decided they would see on their honeymoon. Might be worth a side trip someday, he thought, but now the urge to get to Tioga grew strong within him. The forty mile stretch of absolutely straight road through the barrens west of Seney passed swiftly and soon he saw Lake Superior at Munising. Refueling there, he was amused to hear people talking with the old U.P. accent, prolonging their vowels, saying 'hunt-ting' and 'fissing.' Tom grinned remembering how hard it had been to get that U.P. flavor out of his own speech. Now he would have to learn it again.

He did not remember the highway at all from there to Marquette. There were magnificent stretches that ran along the dunes at the very edge of Lake Superior. There were great hills over which the road swooped into jackpine plains. Finally, he saw the first hills of home, those great granite domes dusted with fir trees, the oldest rocks in the world, people said.

Almost before he knew it, as he turned a hill curve, there was the valley of the Tioga River and the Frenchtown settlement near the depot. But the depot was gone. Up the hill street he drove, his eyes misting as he saw the old house sitting in the big yard. Tom parked the car in the barnyard. The barn was gone and a garage had taken its place. The three apple trees were still in the backyard but they were huge and needed pruning. No outhouse. The big spruce under which he had played in the sandpile as a child had disappeared but the rhubarb patch along the walk still looked lush. Reino had written that the key to the back door would be in the same place - on the ledge above - and it was there, though he'd momentarily forgotten you had to put it in the keyhole upside down. He entered.

Except for the windows, the kitchen was completely strange. No huge range with its woodbox. No pump from the cistern sat on its drainboard. The kitchen cabinet with its large drawers for flour and sugar and utensils no longer stood between the windows. Instead, everything was modern chrome and white. The round kitchen table at which the family had eaten so many meals was gone. Tom was a stranger in a strange room in a strange house. He opened the door to the pantry and closed it quickly again. Exploring further, he found a new bathroom where a closet had been and that the dining and living rooms had been merged into one. The big bookcase and piano were gone. Only the bay window was the same. Suddenly feeling very tired, Tom sat down in a comfortable but strange chair, closing his eyes so he could be for a moment among old memories. He wished he had a stiff drink to lessen the disappointment and loneliness that swept over him.

Finally, Tom shook himself and faced the situation. "No, you can never go back to what you knew fifty-one years ago," he said aloud to himself, lighting his pipe. "So you go forward. You can do anything you want to with this old house once you buy it. So why don't you go up to Reino's house and complete the deal?" After a few more moments, he did so.

Although they were just sitting down to the table, Reino was glad to see him and insisted that Tom have supper with his daughter and her husband. A really warm welcome. Almost like old times eating on an oil-cloth covered kitchen table with happy talk and laughter. It was going to be all right after all. He was back home again. As Tom wrote out the check for the house and signed the papers, Reino said, "Yah, they always come back to the U.P. as soon as they can. Too bad you had to be away so long, Tom. Oh, by the way, did you know that your old sweetheart Mary came back too? About a year ago, she came and she's also living in her old house. Her husband died and her family's grown so she came back too. This is a good place to grow old, Tom. Good hunting and fissing yet. I take you up the Tioga tomorrow, eh? Show you around, eh?"

So Mary had come back too. Tom felt no particular emotion. Indeed he was a bit surprised that there was none. Too long ago! Too many years between. Nevertheless he somehow felt comforted and less lonely. She would be fun to talk to anyway and so would Reino and there would be others. Plenty of things to do. The old house did not seem quite so strange when he returned to sit in the big chair again.

Tom did not sit there long. Up he got and combed his hair and beard. "Gad, what an old man you are!" he said to the image in the mirror. "But she'll be an old woman, too." He crossed the yard and knocked on Mary's door.

A complete stranger, a matronly grey-haired plump woman with eye glasses, opened it. "Yes?" she said, and it was only when he heard her voice that Tom knew it was Mary. "I'm Tom Helet," he replied awkardly. "I've come back too." A look of shock and disbelief came over her face but she invited him in. "Sit down, Tommy, and have a cup of coffee with me. It will be good to talk over old times and get caught up with each other."

The conversation did not flow easily. They found it hard to look at each other. Mary told the story of her life and he told his. Neither seemed particularly interested though they were both very polite. Too polite. After the coffee and cookies were gone, she went to the door with him. "You must come back again, Tommy. Any time." As he turned to leave, he noticed tears in her eyes. "It's been a long, long time," he said, "but it's good to be back."

He crossed his yard and had nearly reached the back door when suddenly he heard her whistle. It was the sodoredo, the sound of the forest bird, the twenty-seventh letter of the alphabet.

NOTHING BUT THE TRUTH

I n that land and at that time with few newspapers and no radio or television, the thing that kept us amused and going was talk. Everything that had happened, was happening, or might be, was constantly discussed in exhaustive detail, spreading from house to house, uphill and down. In such a situation, the person who could tell a good story was prized but only so long as he stuck to something at least vaguely resembling the truth. Slimber Jim Vester was the best story teller in the whole town. Hell, he was the best one in the whole U.P. but he got little honor in our village for he was a congenital and practiced liar. He lied for the love of it.

It wasn't that Slimber Jim stretched the truth, but that he stretched the lie - and without shame. The delight of his life was to find some innocent and then to lead him on and on into an outrage of absurdity as he told his tale. Slimber would lie to anybody but he preferred young boys or traveling salesmen. They were more gullible. He burnt me plenty when I was young, not just once either, but many times. Trouble was he looked and sounded so honest and sincere, what with that shock of white hair and wide innocent blue eyes. Also, he always started off so nice and easy and plausible and the story he would be telling was always so interesting you kept forgetting he was the town liar and couldn't wait for him to finish it. I suppose it's hard for you to understand, not knowing Slimber Jim, but perhaps this sample might help.

With a couple of other kids, I was sitting down in the waiting room at the railway depot passing time till the evening train came in. As usual, there were five or six of the town's unemployed men sitting there talking by the big pot bellied stove. It was either there or Higley's saloon and Higley always booted out anyone who didn't have drinking money.

If I remember right, they were swapping deer hunting stories and a couple of traveling salesmen were listening to them lie when in with his old hound dog came Slimber Jim to stand by the stove facing the salesmen. We kids nudged each other and snickered. We knew what was coming but the old man just stood there benignly, nodding his head in complete belief no matter how wild the tale, and stroking the hound at his feet. Didn't say a word until one of the salemen turned to him and asked if the hound were a good hunter.

"Well," said Slimber, "I can't rightly say yes and I can't say no. Old Grabber here does fair on rabbit give him a trail smoking hot, but for partridge he ain't worth a damn. Well, you can't say that either. If he sees one in a tree, he'll bark some but he don't look up much. Just keeps his nose down snuffing."

"Does he point game?" asked the salesman.

"Naw. Oh, he's got some pointer or setter or springer blood in him, I s'pose, cause he'll freeze a little when he sees a partridge on the ground but he ain't half as good as an old horse I once had."

"A horse that pointed partridge?" The salesman was getting taken.

"Yup. Come by it accidental, but he sure could point pats. Tell you how it happened. Every fall, when partridge season come around, I used to hitch old Joshua up to the buckboard and we'd mozey up them old logging roads back of the dam on the Tioga. Lots of popple there. Good spot for pats, hey Joe?" One of the other men nodded. "Best place around here," he said.

"Well," the old man continued. "We'd be driving along slow like and when I'd see a partridge in the road or in the bushes long side, I'd naturally pull in the reins and then get off the rig and shoot 'im. Well, I do that ten, twelve times, day after day, and pretty soon old Joshua, when he see a partridge, he stop by hisself knowin' I was going to stop him anyway. And, of course, he'd be a-looking at the bird so I could tell whereabouts it was at. Could see 'em better than I could."

"But a good pointer will lift his leg too. Don't suppose your horse would do that?"

"Hell he wouldn't! Joshua just got to stopping quicker and quicker and waiting for me to shoot and pretty soon he'd stop fast on three legs and wave the other one at the bird, he did. Damned smart horse, old Joshua, but not worth a damn on ducks. And he never would retrieve. At that he was better than old Grabber here. And he didn't have fleas either. Don't like fleas. Ain't been able to abide the sight of 'em or lice either. Ever have lice, Mister? No? Well, don't you get a room at the Beacon House up at Ontonogan. I crotched me a mess of 'em there once."

"Thanks," said the salesman. "I'll remember that. How I missed getting them sleeping in some of the Godforsaken hotels on this route I'll never know. How do you get rid of lice if you get them?"

"Well," said Slimber Jim. "It ain't really too hard, you know how. You get one of them fat, two-sided combs with the thin tines and you just keep working your head over, day after day. Better learn how to nick 'em between two finger-nails like this. If you hear 'em make a little pop, you've got 'em. Got to be quick when you get 'em off the comb though. Some of them old graybacks are sure quick legged. They'll be back in yer hair before you can spit. Not too hard to get rid of them but don't try to drown 'em by washing your head. They can swim better than you can. They can't jump though - not like them flea lice I got from Lulu Belle. You happen to know Lulu Belle, Mister?"

"No, can't say I ever knew anybody by that name," said the salesman.

The old man nodded. "Probably not," he said. "She catered more to old men anyway. They didn't mind her wooden leg or the fact that sometimes she was lousy. Used to work out of Green Bay, she did. Come through here maybe once ever two months or so, her and that fleabitten poodle she slept with when she couldn't find her an old gaffer to make happy. . ."

"You said something about flea-lice," interrupted the salesman.

"Yup," said Slimber. "Dunno how it come to be, but Lulu Belle's lice and that damned poodle's flees, they crossbred somehow. Made flice. That's what we come to call 'em hereabouts. Big critters, half an inch long half flea, half lice. Ruined Lulu Belle's trade once they started spreading. You got to watch out for them crossbreeds, Mister. They got the worst parts of both - like the time I mated that there blue heron with a duck. Anyway them flice are blue hell to get rid of. Only one way to do it." Slimber paused, filled and lit his pipe.

"I'm afraid to ask," said the salesman swallowing hard. "How do you get rid of flice?"

"Well, sir," said Slimber. "There's some folks say you can poison 'em and others like to snare them. You sure can't comb 'em out. They jump too good. Had a helluva time till I started studying their habits. Found they feed only on dogs by daylight. Didn't really bite me any time. It was their crawlin' around that bothered - and coming back to sleep in the hair of my crotch at night. Coming back single file. Damned near drove me crazy."

"Well, old man, how did you get rid of them?"

"Waited till after dark and they were bedded down. Then I shaved off all the hair from one side of my crotch, set fire to the other half and stabbed 'em with an ice-pick when they come out of the underbrush."

"Pardon me," said the salesman. "I've got to take my medicine." He opened a bag and took a long swig from a bottle. There was a long pause before he spoke again.

"I think you mentioned, sir, that you had once crossed a blue heron with a duck?" The salesman's voice was respectful.

"Yep. You like chicken meat, Mister? White or dark?"

"I guess I like the dark best. Specially the drumstick."

Slimber Jim put out his hand. "So do I, Mister. Best part of the bird, I say. And that's the worst part of a duck. Not enough drumstick to pick at. Well, sir, I figgered anyone could raise a duck that had good fat drumsticks would make a million dollars. I was living up in a shack by Mud Lake at the time and I tamed me the horniest old blue heron you ever did see. Skinny as a twig he was from screwing every hen heron or thunderpumper around and not finding time enough for fishing. So I give him some of the fish I caught and pretty soon he'd eat it outa my hand, sociable-like.

Well, when you're up in the bush long enough, you keep thinking about beef meat and chicken drumsticks and such after a while and I got the idea to catch me a duck, which I did, and put it in a cage with that old heron hopin' they'd mate. Well, they did, though that old blue heron he has to get down on his knees to get the job done. Them eggs were like none I ever see, Mister. Shaped lopsided and you could hear that she mallard a-yelping every time she laid one. Nine of 'em hatched out too and they growed fast. Funny looking critters they were. Had the long legs of their old man but a short neck like their mother. Full grown, they stood maybe three feet tall. Well, maybe a mite under that, to tell the truth, but they was sure a big awkward bird. Couldn't fly either but Lord Amight, you ought to see them run and jump. Used to jump up and roost on my shack every night. Hell to feed at first cause they couldn't peck up anything on the ground without falling on their face, what with that long legs and short neck and all."

"Were they good eating?" asked the salesman. "Have big drumsticks?"

"Can't tell you, Mister," said Slimber. "Never could catch the buggers. Every morning, they'd lay out a warwhoop and jump down off the shack, then run and jump around the clearing with their mouths open catching flies. Fed on 'em mainly, they did. Cleaned out all the mosquitoes and blackflies and deerflies for three miles around. I could sit outside there by the shack and never have to swat once. Never had it so good. Cleaned them flies up too good cause they kept having to go further and further to feed and when they come back home at night to sleep, they wuz so frazzled they couldn't jump up to roost and then the foxes got 'em. Well, all but one." Slimber paused and emptied his pipe in the pot-bellied stove.

The salesman was silent for a long time, but finally he bit. "What happened to that one?" he asked.

"Well," said Slimber," that one, he was the best jumper of the bunch. Choked to death on a woodpecker." The salesman grabbed up his bags and fled into the night.

CULLY GAGE

"Cully Gage" was born December 1, 1905, the son of an Upper Peninsula family physician and his wife. It could be said that he was a "child of the forest", for as a very young lad he loved exploring the forests with all of its' trails and trout streams. He was familiar with nearly every acre of land from Champion north to Lake Superior.

The name Cully Gage is the pen name for one of the most common, genuine, sincere and down-to-earth men it has ever been our pleasure to know. He explained to us that as a boy, the Finns called him "Kalle", their word for Carl or Charles, and his middle name was Gage after his "marvelous grandfather". His given name is Dr. Charles Gage VanRiper but inside he has always been "Cully Gage".

After spending the early years of his life with the people he writes about and when civilization beset him, he took the train from his home town to Marquette where he enrolled at Northern Michigan University. He studied at Northern for two years and then transferred to the University of Michigan in Ann Arbor where he earned his Bachelor of Arts and Master of Arts degrees, subsequently teaching in the high schools of both Saline and Champion.

From childhood "Cully" had been plagued with a frustrating speech problem and determined to conquer it, he enrolled at the University of Iowa where he completed his Ph. D. and not only found a surcease to his own difficulties but also a new and challenging field. He returned to Michigan and began teaching at Western Michigan University in Kalamazoo.

In 1936 he established the Speech Clinic at Western Michigan University providing help and correction for many "faltering tongues". He has authored numerous text books dealing with the causes and correction of speech difficulties. "Cully" worked very closely with many of his students helping them to overcome the anxieties of hesitant speaking. Many of his students have not only lived in his home but have also helped him plant pine trees at more than one cabin site. They were introduced to the serenity of the woodlands and streams of the northland by this fine man.

Now in semi-retirement he shares two beautiful worlds; the "forest child" has a 122 year old farmhouse in downstate Portage where he has a large organic garden and is striving to produce his Perfect Potatoes. He has developed a beautiful park on the land surrounding the house and 30 foot pine trees planted as seedlings grace the area. He also maintains a special retreat in the Upper Peninsula of Michigan. His wife Catharine, their three kids and nine grandkids all share in his feeling for both where carpets of pine needles and love abound.

For all who know and admire Cully Gage, that certain twinkle of mischief in his eyes will always be present and his stories of early life in the great Upper Peninsula will provide hours of entertainment and reminiscing.

We wish to take this opportunity to thank Cully for sharing his stories of those great people and events which were such an integral part of his early life in the land he loves so much. By allowing us to record them on paper they will be remembered and enjoyed forever.

Avery Color Studios

Sue Krill

Sue Krill, the illustrator, is the daughter of Cully Gage. She is the mother of four children, teaches flute, aerobic dancing and, although she has long been painting, these are her first pen and ink sketches. Although now a native of Grand Haven, Michigan she too loves the Upper Peninsula and has managed to visit there every year of her life.

The first Northwoods Reader is a 120 page, beautifully illustrated, soft cover volume which paints a vivid picture of life in the northwoods, of a lifestyle and the colorful characters most of us remember — and wish we'd written about.

— from "The Chivaree" — one of 18 great stories in CULLY GAGE'S FIRST NORTHWOODS READER.

They had worked out an arrangement whereby Old Man Putinen delivered milk and butter to a number of customers in town while Aili did the milking and churning. They also had some joint chickens and the old man sold the eggs.

It was a sensible economic arrangement, but it stimulated a lot of gossipy clack about how far the sharing really went. Even the preacher suggested, gently of course, that they might be wise to get married if only to put a stop to all the bad talk.

Aili and Putinen both rejected the outrageous suggestion immediately. They were just friends.

Old Putinen said he didn't believe in all that ceremonial stuff anyway, with licenses and everything. Said he'd never bought a license in his life for hunting or fishing or anything else. Said he'd fathered seven children by his first wife without a license and was damned if he'd start now with all that nonsense.

Besides, he said, he wasn't about to put out any good money on any damned chivaree.

Putinen and Aili were both known for being tight. She reportedly saved her coffee grounds, drying them and putting them back in the can until they were completely blond. . . even after she shook them.

She wore shoepacks to church and they tell of the time she asked the butcher to cut the cheese with a ham knife: "I dearly love the flavor of ham," she said.

They were both very frugal!